Living a
Spiritual Life
in a
Material
World

Living a Spiritual Life in a Material World

Four Keys to Fulfillment and Balance

Anna Gatmon, PhD

SHE WRITES PRESS

Published 2017
Printed in the United States of America
Print ISBN: 978-1-63152-256-7
E-ISBN: 978-1-63152-257-4
Library of Congress Control Number: 2017938527

For information, address:
She Writes Press
1563 Solano Ave #546
Berkeley, CA 94707

Cover and interior design by Tabitha Lahr

She Writes Press is a division of SparkPoint Studio, LLC.

To all who wish for heaven on earth.
Together, we can make it happen.

Contents

Section I

Reclaiming Your Spiritual Birthright............1

1. What Does Your Soul Long For?.................3
2. A Journey Towards Wholeness.................11
3. What if God Was One of Us? 23

Section II

The Four Keys to Spiritual–Material Balance...35

4. Expansive Presence: The Key to
   Sacred Awareness............................37
5. Attentive Listening: The Key to
   Inner Wisdom 55
6. Inspired Action: The Key to
   Manifesting................................69

7. Faith-Filled Knowing: The Key to

   Ongoing Co-Creation 85

Section III

Accelerating Your Spiritual Development 97

   8. The Four Keys Come Together 99

   9. Dedicating Yourself to Practicing the

      Four Keys. 107

   10. Finding Wholeness Through the

       Unity in Nature 115

   11. Aspire to Spiritual–Material Balance 123

   Epilogue: You're Off to Great Places 127

*The goal is not
to lose oneself in
the Divine Consciousness.
The goal is to let the
Divine Consciousness
penetrate into matter
and transform it.*

—The Mother

Section I

Reclaiming Your
Spiritual Birthright

Chapter 1

What Does Your Soul Long For?

All my life I have experienced a profound longing to have access to a hidden world, a place where everything is possible and the rules of being are different than those of our earthly existence. In this hidden reality my life is sacred; I am loved and appreciated and attended to with care. I feel special and have been given a unique role to make our planet a better place. To do this, infinite wisdom becomes available to me through loving guidance, providing me with the power to change the course of my life and that of others.

While the clarity of this longing has evolved over the years, I had a visceral experience of it the moment I entered this world. The split between this hidden dimension and my earthly existence happened at the time of my birth. I have a vivid memory of being born—a small, precious, and whole baby coming out of my mother's womb into a room of cold neon light. I felt immediately separated from a part of me that was hovering above the sterile stainless-steel surfaces of the hospital. This part emanated boundless love and a sense of eternal unity beyond physical existence. And ever since, I have felt a longing to be reunited with this timeless and infinite aspect of my being.

While this longing has been accompanied by moments of loneliness, despair, and feelings of having been forsaken, it has also propelled me in wondrous directions, far beyond my personal and cultural upbringing. This longing has become my guide and compass— my means to finding my way back home to the hidden world within me.

You may also feel in your heart a longing for some deeper purpose and greater meaning for your life. It may keep you up at night wondering whether you will ever find true fulfillment. But it may also direct you to positive life experiences that you might never otherwise seek. Like me, you may find that certain inner promptings urge you to keep growing, moving you further along a mindful path towards a significant life.

A Response to this Longing

About ten years ago I attended a talk given by His Holiness the Dalai Lama. During the Q&A segment a young woman raised her hand and asked a question that I myself had been grappling with for several years: "We go to many workshops," she said, "read books on spirituality, and are introduced to many spiritual teachings, but how do we apply all these in our daily living?"

The Dalai Lama's answer was that continuing education is key to integrating spiritual teachings into our daily life. This includes ongoing self-inquiry regarding our spiritual nature, examining what supports and what hinders us from experiencing our spiritual magnitude, and then integrating our findings into our material existence. It was a response that came from an awakened and self-realized perspective. The woman's question, however, came from a place of struggle; she, like most of us, perceived the spiritual and material aspects of her life as belonging to different realms.

For example, you might go to a meditation retreat where you have wonderful meditative experiences. You'd love to bring the peace and relaxation you experienced during the retreat into your life, but find it challenging to access it once you return home and are sucked into the seemingly endless demands of to-do lists. Or perhaps you have come across a great book filled with spiritual wisdom with which you deeply resonate, but you don't know how to apply these teachings to the nitty-gritty of daily living.

Many of us fail to see that our spiritual life is not limited to time spent in church or temple. Instead of recognizing that it is also present in the work we do, the relationships we have, and our overall engagement with the world around us, we have developed false notions that create a split between what we call "spiritual" and what we call "material." Consenting to cultural norms, we have accepted the false perception that the spiritual and the material aspects of life are separate.

The Four Keys to spiritual–material balance that I share in this book—Expansive Presence, Attentive Listening, Inspired Action, and Faith-Filled Knowing—can help mend this spiritual–material split. They provide a method for accessing inner spiritual dimensions and applying them to external material living. They are rooted in the reality that we each have the capacity to connect with the Divine within us and within everything around us. They go right to the heart of sacred universal experiences and can therefore be applied across diverse religious and spiritual practices.

The Four Keys will help you share your unique spirit more fully and support your spiritual development in a very practical, hands-on way. Practicing the Four Keys will deepen your connection to the spiritual dimension of your life and show you how to bring out your distinctive spiritual gifts. You will develop your innate capacity for inner guidance and learn how to manifest your full potential as a spiritual being, so that you can live a fulfilling and purposeful life—one that is spiritually guided yet grounded in your daily material living.

Here are some immediate and long-term benefits you can expect to experience when using the Four Keys:

- Get out of a dispirited mood within minutes

- Shift from feeling alone in the world to feeling that you are cared for and guided by a loving Universe

- Enhance your impact on daily situations

- Develop your intuitive decision-making skills

- Gain practical tools for manifesting your true and authentic self

- Feel passionately engaged in expressing your unique divine purpose

- Find a greater sense of harmony, intimacy, and connection with people

- Lead an overall healthier physical, emotional, mental, and spiritual life.

Whether you have just begun your conscious spiritual journey or have been on the path for quite some time, using the Four Keys will help accelerate your spiritual development. However, there are three attitudes that will prevent you from experiencing the beneficial impact of the Four Keys:

I knew that already: If what you come across in this book is familiar to you, rather than dismissing it, use it to take your spiritual practice to the next level and delve deeper into your divine self. The simplest teachings are often the hardest to integrate.

I disagree: Don't get caught up in the "this or that" of dualistic thinking. Every spiritual teaching highlights a different aspect of our divine nature, and no one teaching can encompass the magnitude of the Eternal Reality. The Four Keys offer a glimpse into that reality and focus specifically on how to live a spiritually guided life that is grounded in daily living.

It's not going to work for me: Whether you are longing for just a bit more happiness and inner peace or full spiritual enlightenment, give the Four Keys a chance; practicing them is sure to advance you towards your goal.

Expressing your divine self requires a willingness to let go of old and constricting concepts of God and open up to new and expansive experiences of your divinity. This is not always an easy journey to undertake, as self-doubt, personal history, and collective conventions may cast shadows on your path. But it is a journey worth taking, filled with adventure and opportunities for learning and growing. It is a magical journey of liberation from that which keeps you small and seemingly safe—one that will carry you towards greater wholeness and a peace-filled, prosperous, and purposeful life.

Whether you are on a conscious spiritual journey or are not yet fully aware of your spiritual nature, this book will strengthen the connection to your divinity and provide you with tools to enhance your unique expression in the world.

Chapter 2

A Journey Towards Wholeness

I grew up with a Jewish Israeli father and Swedish Protestant Christian mother. This meant that until I converted in my early thirties I was not officially Jewish. Growing up in Israel in a Jewish culture and being the only family of mixed religion was a cause for a lot of embarrassment and shame. I also had red hair and freckles—a look that was not very popular at the time—and stuttered heavily, a gene I'd inherited from my mother's side of the family. So I spent my childhood feeling like an inadequate outsider.

My parents were quite different from each other. My father was very strict, punitive, and shaming, and my mother submissive and overly lenient. My father's opening bid was always "no," while my mother could never say "no" to any request I made. My father was a pilot, and as such would be gone for days at a time, leaving my mother, a homemaker, to raise us according to her rules and rhythm. Each time my father returned, the pace would change. I tried hard to anticipate and adjust to these varying and oppositional parenting styles, trying to make sense of the extreme fluctuations of restrictions, but it wasn't easy. And on top of all that, my mother was an alcoholic and my father was prone to fits of rage. I found myself experiencing disrespect towards my mother and living in fear of my father.

Unfortunately, school wasn't a relief from the challenging situation at home—in fact, my memories of both elementary and high school are characterized by feelings of low self-esteem and inadequacy. I was sure I was stupid because I found the standard lecture form of teaching very challenging, doing homework tedious, and taking exams stressful. I felt my life, both at home and at school, was out of control.

When I was thirteen my parents separated and my mother moved back to Sweden, where she sought professional help for her drinking. Meanwhile, my younger siblings and I moved in with my father and his new partner. Those teenage years in a new family constellation were not easy. I was lonely and felt overwhelmed by my unresolved emotional issues.

Relief finally came when I finished high school and was allowed to travel to Sweden to visit my mother, whom I hadn't seen for a while. Once there, I took summer courses to improve my Swedish, which necessitated my living independently of my mom. I loved the freedom and sense of selfhood I found in this new life, making new friends and learning to find my own way in the world.

My luck changed dramatically when a fashion-modeling scout approached me one Saturday morning while I was waiting in line at a local store. One thing led to another, and four months later I found myself traveling to Paris, France to try my luck as a fashion model. I began working within a few weeks and decided to stay and live in Paris. After years of feeling trapped and hopeless, I finally felt free from the tyranny of my childhood: my mother's drinking and my father's dominance.

I can still feel the sense of excitement and new possibility I experienced during this time. This relatively sudden shift of fate offered me the important understanding that life could change for the better in an instant. Many times since then, when I have found myself at a crossroads in life, I have used this visceral memory as a resource.

As a fashion model for a decade in both Europe and the United States, I did print work for the biggest magazines, runway shows with leading designers, advertising on billboards, and commercials on TV. I traveled to exciting locations around the world for many of the photo shoots, was chosen to be the face for one of the

Yves Saint Laurent perfumes, and even got to meet Steven Spielberg when he was scouting for the lead female role for *Indiana Jones and the Temple of Doom*.

Working as a fashion model turned out to be my ticket to freedom—but I was still hampered by my childhood trauma, which I had not yet addressed. In spite of all the glamorous attention I was receiving, I was filled with insecurity and self-criticism.

Throughout this time, my mother's alcoholism continued. At some point, however, she tried rehab again, and as part of supporting her I was introduced to the addictions recovery movement. My Parisian life as a model became interspersed with attending twelve-step program meetings—Al-Anon and Adult Children of Alcoholics (ACOA) for dealing with having grown up in an alcoholic family, and Food Addicts Anonymous (FA) for my anorexic tendencies. Within a few meetings, I discovered a void I had not previously acknowledged.

So much of my life had changed for the better: I was financially independent, had been in a few serious relationships, and had built myself a satisfying life in Paris. And yet the old longing, deep and persistent, reasserted its power. I realized I still yearned for deeper meaning and greater purpose and harbored a desire for connection and community. In twelve-step meetings I felt whole, a part of something greater than the material life I was leading. As I shared my story of suffering and addiction, I discovered ways to let go of my past and begin healing.

I began shifting from a state of internal victimhood to a sense of mental and emotional freedom.

This was the first step on my journey towards living a conscious spiritual life, though I didn't know it yet; those meetings talked about the importance of developing a relationship with a Higher Power, but I didn't categorize my experience as spiritual. Nonetheless, my journey towards wholeness had begun. I decided to leave the world of fashion and go back to school. I also met my husband at that time and moved to the United States, where I received my doctoral degree in Transformative Learning, a holistic discipline that introduced me to supportive and empowering educational practices. Still, it took another fifteen years of self-inquiry and personal growth before the Four Keys revealed themselves to me.

Finding the Path Back Home

My spiritual journey evolved slowly and revealed itself gradually without my paying much attention. I was in my early forties when I finally realized a significant spiritual dimension had been integral to my existence throughout my life. By that time, I had been married for ten years and had two young boys who filled my life with joy and unconditional love. I had spent over a decade participating in different self-empowerment workshops and women's circles, and had read many self-help books. All of these experiences had helped peel away the layers of personal suffering and cultural conditioning I had amassed over the years; I felt I was now living a healthy physical and emotional lifestyle.

Three major areas of my life had come into a viable and satisfying balance. I had moved from starving my emotions through anorexia to eating more consciously and expressing my feelings in a healthy way. Instead of falling for men who were unavailable like my father had been, I chose to marry a loving man who was willing to grow, both as an individual and, with me, as a couple. And I chose to homeschool my children according to my own educational beliefs, instead of sending them to public school. I was on a conscious journey towards wholeness—my personal wholeness, my children's wholeness, and my family's wholeness.

And yet that old longing to access a hidden world remained. I wanted to transcend my ordinary and mundane life and enter into an enchanted and exalted world. Ever since my mother had read magical tales to me as a child, I had longed to connect with the veiled world of elemental beings described in those stories—beings that had magical powers to support our material existence. I also wanted God to take the time to speak to me personally, as he did to Moses through the burning bush, though I never shared that secret desire with anyone. I wished to have the compassionate nature of Jesus; I wanted to live in this world without being dragged down by emotional turmoil, either my own or that of others. I longed for the sweet simplicity of attaining enlightenment while sitting under a tree, just as the Buddha had after trying in vain to reach enlightenment through austere suffering.

Perhaps likening myself to Moses, Jesus, or the Buddha seems arrogant, but I believe that most of us seekers yearn in our deepest hearts to be like those magnificent exemplars. Ultimately, this longing was answered through a life-changing event: a workshop I attended that focused on developing an unmediated relationship of love, inspiration, and guidance with a personal God.

The workshop's facilitator made what seemed to me a bold claim: "Each one of us can have direct contact with the Divine by attuning ourselves to the subtle inner dimensions of our being." One specific exercise was pivotal to the radical shift in my understanding of how accessible and intimate God is to every one of us. The exercise began with a guided meditation. The facilitator led us into a relaxed state of quiet breathing and then asked that we identify three specific moments in our lives.

"First," the facilitator suggested, "recall a time when you experienced a sense of transcendence."

I picked the powerful poem "The Road Not Taken" by Robert Frost. Reading it always connects me to an exalted state of higher knowing and guides me to the road "less traveled" when I reach crossroads in my life. As I recalled the poem, I could feel warm tingling vibrations in my hands, chest, and belly, and a strong sense of purpose and calling.

The facilitator continued, "Now, remember an instance when you felt in awe of the beauty in nature."

I chose a small, seemingly insignificant maple tree outside the workshop building. Each time I went by it, I'd stop to look at its fiery red leaves stretching into the autumn cool. Its beauty cracked my heart open, transporting me to an existence beyond time and space, where everything around me seemed to recede into the background.

"Finally," the facilitator concluded, "pick a situation where you basked in the loving presence of another person."

I chose my younger son, age five at the time. Thinking of him brought a smile to my face and joy to my heart. I felt flooded with love remembering his little hands touching me, the scent of his head, and the feel of his hugs.

All three experiences evoked a sense of awe and surrender to the present moment.

What a powerful guided meditation!

At the end of this exercise, the facilitator concluded, "The particular experiences you've chosen in this meditation, and the qualities you've identified, are a doorway to your inner divinity, your direct connection to the spiritual realm."

This astounded me. The meditation was similar to many other exercises I had done over the past fifteen years of my journey towards wholeness, and yet the thought that the doorway to the spiritual realm was so accessible and readily available surprised me. Until that moment, I had never considered a relationship with a personal God to be an option. Connecting with God, I thought, was the privilege of those who adhered to a particular faith and rigorously practiced a specific religion. As I was living a secular life, there was no way that I would be given the privilege to speak directly to God.

With the realization that Spirit was so accessible came the understanding that I had been living a spiritual life all along—without knowing it. This meant that I had experienced many spiritual moments throughout my life without having recognized their spiritual nature.

As the days went by, I began to understand that the sense of peace and joy I felt when taking in the scent of wet earth after rain was a spiritual experience; that the sense of elation I felt during bursts of creativity was a spiritual experience; and my heart bursting with love and gratitude as I lay next to my children at night, helping them to fall asleep, was a spiritual experience as well. I also recognized that if such daily occurrences were of a spiritual nature, other people were also having similar experiences while going about their daily lives.

Since then, I have come to realize that none of us needs to be a Moses, Jesus, or the Buddha to have a personal relationship with the Divine. We are all chosen and have the capacity to access our inner divinity at any time throughout our day. The problem is, we don't always recognize that it's happening.

Discovering the Four Keys to
Spiritual–Material Balance

I began to practice connecting with my inner divinity on a daily basis. Each time I thought I was having a spiritual experience, I would check for any shifts in sensations, trying to identify where in my body I was feeling the shift. I would identify feelings associated with the moment and pay attention to significant changes in my thought patterns. As I studied the nature of my spirituality, these subtle shifts became my cues for spiritual experiences. They helped me identify and intensify such daily experiences—and, as I realized that I could choose to engage in specific activities that were more prone to evoke in me a spiritual state of mind, they helped me create those experiences on demand. Just as I had done in the guided meditation in the workshop, I could read a poem that moved me or spend time in the presence of trees in order to intentionally enter into a spiritual state of being.

As I delved deeper into my spiritual inquiry, I discovered the Four Keys to spiritual–material balance, which became the focus of my doctoral dissertation. These keys, Expanded Presence, Attentive Listening, Inspired Action, and Faith-Filled Knowing, offer a perfect balance between the sacred and the mundane, the spiritual and the material. Using the Four Keys encourages us to go inward into metaphysical realms and retrieve wisdom and guidance that we can apply in our practical material life. They invite us to perceive and appreciate the spiritual nature of our daily existence and the material expression of our spiritual intentions, creating a unity and balance between our material and spiritual existence.

We're almost ready to dive into the description and practice of each key, but before we do, let's take a moment to talk about the nature of spirituality and what it means to have an intimate relationship with God, Spirit, or the Universe.

Chapter 3

What if God Was One of Us?

Suppose we could simplify spirituality and make it accessible to everyone. Then we would all be able to access our innate spiritual capacities and experience everything we do in our daily life as having a spiritual component. After all, the spiritual dimension of our being is an innate part of our human nature; it's not just a gift bestowed on the sages and mystics that have graced our planet throughout history, but is an enhanced perspective available to all of us. In fact, it is our birthright.

The truth is, while the source of our spiritual nature may forever remain indescribable, there is a lot about spirituality that is definable, practical, and accessible to anyone. It requires retraining certain muscles and developing greater precision with our language, but it is doable—and the results can be immediate.

Are you ready? Let's begin!

You know the feeling: you're flying in a plane, and suddenly there is turbulence and everything is shaking, with the plane bouncing up and down. It can be unpleasant and even scary! To get out of turbulent air, the pilots often climb to a higher altitude, where the atmosphere is calm, and then everything settles down again. Well, that is what spirituality is all about—rising to a higher altitude of emotional and mental stability where there is no turbulence and your being can sail over the disturbances of daily life with greater ease. When you act in the world from a higher spiritual altitude, the answers to challenges reflect your most noble intentions, providing creative, innovative, and compassionate solutions.

Tapping into a spiritual reality is really about rising to an altitude where you gain a larger perception of the world with all its opportunities and challenges. The higher you rise spiritually, the more encompassing your perspective on any given situation becomes. What separates you and me from mystics, prophets, and sages is that they naturally reside for long periods of time in this expansive spiritual altitude and therefore have access to higher, otherworldly truths that can transform our earthly reality. The Four Keys are an accessible and readily available roadmap to a higher spiritual plane, allowing us to integrate its wisdom and guidance into our worldly daily living and to inhabit this all-inclusive awareness for longer and more sustained periods of time.

What's God Got to Do With It?

What is your concept of the ultimate unfathomable, transcendent force? Is it an old man with a white beard who sits on his throne with a staff and keeps score of your sins? This is the Judeo-Christian concept of God with which many of us grew up. Alternatively, you may refer to this force as Spirit and experience it not so much as a Supreme Being but as the creative love that flows through everything around, from stone, plant, and animal to humans. Then again, you may have given up altogether on believing there is more to life than what you can experience with your five senses, yet you remain in awe of the natural world and are a person of great moral values and integrity—you've just never thought of these as being parts of the spiritual dimension of your being.

However you choose to relate to this transcendent force, all spiritual traditions speak of a hidden intelligence of endless potential and creativity from which everything seems to originate, and into which everything dissolves. This infinite force, spoken of as both the source and end of everything, has been given different names in different spiritual and religious traditions: God, Goddess, Jehovah,

Allah, Great Spirit, Cosmic Love, Higher Power, Divine Source, Brahman, the Light, the Eternal, and many more. Some of these terms refer to an entity or a being, while others refer to a realm or field of consciousness. Different names may fit different contexts, as well as offer different aspects of the essence and nature of this inconceivable reality. For example, in Hinduism, Brahma is God as the creator entity, while Brahman is the consciousness of God as it permeates all beings. The Goddess is the ultimate Divine force, conceived of through feminine principles, while the Source or the Eternal are gender- and culture-neutral. My preference is to relate to this force as the Universe, a loving Universe, or a loving and creative Universe, but I do use different terms at different times throughout this book in order to describe and evoke different qualities of this field of consciousness. By doing so, I am also attempting to avoid limiting its expression to any particular cultural or religious association.

Regardless of the term used, I believe there is a general understanding of what is implied: an infinite dimension that we humans experience as the Sacred and the Divine within ourselves and in everything around us, be it nature, people, events, or our actions and deeds. Many moments in our daily lives reveal to us this sacred divinity: the sense of peace and wholeness triggered by a walk in nature or the scent of fresh herbs; being washed with love and warmth after receiving the look or touch of a child; a feeling of gratitude while cooking a wholesome meal for ourselves or others; a sense of truth and clarity when we find ourselves in the right place at the right time, doing what we consider the right thing; experiencing elation and inspiration during creative expression; or that sense of inner joy and contentment we feel when our life is filled with a purpose that serves a higher good. This is the tangible and measurable part of spirituality that we have all experienced at some point, and probably quite often, in our lives. These seemingly mundane situations offer a personal and unmediated access to the Divine and the Sacred and are available to each of us at any given moment.

Whatever beliefs you may have grown up with or hold today regarding your own divinity and the Spirit that permeates everything, I am sure that you have experienced moments of joy, peace, contentment, compassion, love, beauty, inspiration, and intuitive insight. These are moments when our spirit awakens and we find deeper meaning, purpose, connection, wholeness, inner joy, and contentment in daily activities and tasks with which we engage. We may not always be aware of the sacred nature of these ordinary activities, but nevertheless, during such moments, we transcend our habitual perspective on life and experience the world and ourselves from a higher, more appreciative awareness. In this higher plane, we literally expand our consciousness, free ourselves from habitual constraints, and allow love, bliss, and our full power to flow more freely through our being.

As a result, a deep connection with another person can be experienced as an intense spiritual experience; a creative burst during a team meeting can feel like we are "in the zone," hooked into a plane of higher inspiration; and smelling the earth after the rain while taking our daily walk can give us a sense of openness and joy at being an integral part of nature.

Sometimes, spiritual experiences are of a mystical nature, such as near-death experiences, sensing the presence of a being of love and light, or connecting with someone who has passed away. However, most spiritual experiences are part of our everyday lives and may occur at any moment. They are not reserved solely for visits to church, temple, or the meditation mat. They occur while we work and go about daily activities, interacting with the world in a seemingly mundane fashion.

Spiritual Seekers

Whether you adhere to a specific religion, follow your self-created spiritual path, or recognize your spiritual nature without believing in a supreme force, you probably fall somewhere in between two categories: the *determined seeker* and the *ambivalent seeker*. These comprise two ends of a spectrum that contains many individual variations.

It is a common cliché among people in general, and spiritual seekers in particular, that a truly spiritual person ultimately rejects material possessions and doesn't indulge in material pleasures. In this idealized view, the genuinely spiritual live a simple, humble life, with no desire to possess material goods or experience material gratification.

This misconception is due to an artificial division of our life into the sacred and the mundane, the spiritual and the material. In this dualistic view of reality, determined seekers are willing to give up material possessions for the promise of spiritual enlightenment. Ambivalent seekers, in contrast, acknowledge the reality of our material existence and don't trust that adopting a purely spiritual perspective will pay the bills and take care of them in old age.

Both determined and ambivalent seekers end up feeling spiritually inadequate—determined seekers because they haven't yet attained spiritual enlightenment but are experiencing less material comfort, and ambivalent seekers because they feel short-changed as they hold on to their material security without access to some greater spiritual fulfillment. This kind of thinking leaves most of us mortals outside the spiritual playing field.

Whether you identify more with the ambivalent or the determined seeker, most of our daily living consists of engaging with the material world. A more integrated and less compartmentalized perspective can help us mend the spiritual–material split, offering a way to make peace with our inevitable material existence while experiencing greater meaning and purpose in our daily living.

Integrating the Mundane and the Sacred

It seems we have taken the sacred out of most of our modern life. For example, we produce, consume, and discard food without stopping to appreciate the wonder of seeds that turn into trees that bear fruit that nourishes our bodies and souls. Isn't a perfect peach or an apple a miracle of ingenuity and an expression of earthly delight? Isn't golden wheat blowing in the wind—and our craft of turning it into bread—a nourishing and creative collaboration between nature and humans? And yet we have trivialized this sacred interdependence, ravaging nature for our personal benefit and treating food as a commodity.

In much the same way, we go through life checking off items on our to-do lists without a thought given to daily opportunities for spiritual growth and transformation in our work environment. We are even willing to give up essential aspects of our being in order to fulfill job expectations, instead of treating the work we do in the world as an opportunity to express our love, dedication, expertise, service, and creativity. From the time we start attending school, we are taught to give up our emotional, spiritual, and creative essence and replace them with rote learning, competitiveness, and survival mechanisms. We all suffer, teachers and students alike, from this splitting of ourselves, from cutting off essential aspects of our being, from being forbidden to be vulnerable, creative, or soulful. Schooling seems to focus mostly on accumulating knowledge, passing exams, and getting good grades, instead of valuing experiential learning, practicing emotional intelligence to deal with social interactions, and honoring the creative inner life of children.

In a similar manner, we don't often think of the people we care for most as secret spiritual teachers who help us grow and learn—our children, for example, who teach us the most important and challenging lessons in life about loving and being loved unconditionally. Instead, we often treat our parenting role as a task to produce a successful human being who adheres to societal and cultural norms. If you've ever spent time just hanging out with your kids instead of trying to get through the daily list of chores, then you know how insightful they can be and how much we adults can learn from their candid perception.

These are all illustrations of daily situations in which we have separated the sacred from the mundane and split the spiritual from the material. Yet all these examples are both material and spiritual: The peach, in and of itself, is material, but the experience of consuming it and enjoying it is an internal experience that gives us access to the emotional and spiritual realms of our existence. The work we do in the world is filled with material actions that need to happen in order to accomplish daily tasks and goals, and yet a shift in our attitude can change a tedious to-do list into an experience of a higher calling and purpose. And hugging our children is a material experience that provides emotional and spiritual satisfaction. Actually, any and every situation can be experienced as being composed of both material and spiritual components.

A shift in our awareness and consequent perspective can turn a seemingly mundane material situation into a sacred, spiritual experience. This can happen when we begin to see each aspect of our lives as sacred, no matter how small the task with which we are engaged. Anything we do quite obviously involves a material, physical component, but through a subtle shift in our perception the sacred divinity of each activity and situation can also be revealed, allowing us to experience greater meaning and higher purpose in our daily lives.

Picture an executive business meeting that begins with each person choosing a meaningful quality they would like to practice during the meeting; an environmental policy summit that starts with a hike in the wilderness; or a public school teacher starting the day with a meditation where he envisions his students as beautiful souls who long to be seen and valued. You can imagine the qualitative shift in such sessions, the expansion of everyone's consciousness, the enjoyable work and study environment, and the inspired and creative solutions to problems and challenges. Just envision how much more gratifying and fulfilling life would be and what kind of transformational impact such practices, when applied on a larger scale, would have on our planet.

The Four Keys can provide such a qualitative shift. They help mend the spiritual–material split by addressing both aspects and integrating them into daily living. They offer a roadmap to the seemingly hidden spiritual dimension of daily living and propose concrete ways of manifesting the sacred in our material existence.

Section II

The Four Keys to
Spiritual-Material Balance

Chapter 4

Expansive Presence:

The Key to Sacred Awareness

Have you ever looked at a flower and felt great appreciation for its beauty? Do stories about people's courage in the face of adversity move you and renew your hope in humanity? Is there something you enjoy doing so much that it gives you an exhilarated sense of purpose?

We have all experienced appreciation, hope, and purpose in the most ordinary circumstances while going through our daily routine. When we do, we are transported to a higher and more noble, spiritual part of ourselves. What makes it "spiritual" is an inherent characteristic of expansiveness that occurs to varying degrees, whether we are aware of it or not.

The first key, Expansive Presence, involves making a conscious effort to identify and become aware of expansive moments in our daily lives, moments when our spirit awakens and taps into a vaster spiritual reality. Once we are able to identify such instances, we can practice enhancing them and even creating them intentionally on demand. While spiritual experiences are highly personal and subjective, they all result in tangible shifts and notable changes in our bodily sensations, emotions, and thoughts.

Expansive Sensations

The sensation associated with spiritual experiences is one of expanding beyond the boundaries of your physical body. If, for example, you are experiencing a sense of grounding, then you will feel that you are extending beyond your legs and feet and are blending into the supporting floor or earth. If you are experiencing a sense of elation, then you may very well sense an extension of your being beyond the contours of your torso and arms into the space surrounding you. This expansive fluidity alters your relationship to all things, and you begin to see and experience everything as being more alive and interconnected. You become aware of greater subtleties in your bodily sensations, which in turn provide you with valuable information about your present experience.

Living in a culture that primarily values mind over body, it is sometimes challenging to identify bodily sensations of expansiveness. And yet these sensations are powerful cues for recognizing and enhancing spiritual experiences. They may manifest in a specific area of the body and involve an increase in the flow of energy to that particular part—for example, a heart opening might be experienced as expansiveness in the chest. Or they may present themselves more generally as an overall sensation of well-being—for example, experiencing a sense of warmth washing over you. One woman I worked with would recognize her entry into an expansive state by an accompanying tingling in her nose. Another person would experience the hair on his arms standing on end. Any change in sensation anywhere in your body is an indication that your being is expanding beyond your normal perception of yourself. Trust it!

Expansive Emotions

The overarching emotional state of spiritual experiences is one of self-love and the love of others, which can be felt and expressed through many different feelings. Whether you feel kinder, more caring and compassionate, peaceful, joyful, or inspired, these feelings are all expressions of greater love and reverence towards yourself and others. It may be clear that caring for your elderly parent is an act of love and compassion. Feeling inspired during a burst of creativity is a less obvious example, but it is an act of self-love that requires your expansiveness to allow greater wisdom to come through you. As you allow for that wisdom to come through your unique personality and capabilities, it becomes an act of self-care.

In contrast, when you are experiencing supposedly negative feelings—for example, envy—it is not an act of self-love but of emotional self-hurt. Envy and resentment constrict your consciousness instead of expanding it. When you are envious of someone and want something they have—something you perceive yourself as lacking—you are by definition denying its existence in you. But the truth is, you would not even have taken note of someone else having that thing if it did not already exist in you; it is something you already possess, but in the form of a denied or dormant longing that you have avoided or ignored in some way. Whether or not you are conscious of this longing, seeing it in another awakens it in you.

If you instead reframe your resentment as a desire to connect to that part in you that you perceive in someone else, then you will have turned a constricting emotion into an agent of expansion. Now you can take full responsibility for your own yearning and do what it takes to fulfill it. For example, envying the financial freedom of a friend constricts your consciousness, because it makes you feel inadequate by comparison. In contrast, however, if you recognize that you are yearning for the underlying freedom that you believe money can provide, you can either come up with a concrete plan of attaining financial increase, create more free time for a hobby that you enjoy, or dedicate more time to hanging out with family and friends. With this reframe, the person you envied a moment ago becomes a messenger from your soul, reminding you to listen to that which is calling you from within and propelling you to grow and expand.

Expansive Thoughts

Thoughts that may enter your mind while you're experiencing expansion involve a more inclusive perspective on any given situation. For example, if you are stressed about a deadline at work, you might choose to take a break and listen to your favorite music. As the music carries you, you let go of the stressful and constricted state and flow into a more relaxed and expansive one. Your thoughts will no longer be trapped in worry, and instead may roam towards more efficient ways to work towards your deadline. These more expansive thoughts might offer a specific strategy to a problem you encountered with your work, or inspire an original idea on how to lower your stress level while facing your deadline. Paying attention to such expansive thoughts allows you to gain a more spacious perspective on your situation.

A good metaphor for moving from constricted to expansive thinking is the scale of the map you use to navigate from one place to another. Let's say you are in a large city and are using a GPS to find your way. If you look at the virtual map on your smartphone, you are shown only a very small segment of the route you need to take, which makes it difficult to grasp the relationship between where you are and where you want to go. In contrast, if you are able to look at a map that shows the entire city, then you discover the connection and relationship between its different districts.

The same occurs as your consciousness expands during a spiritual experience. You gain a larger perspective and begin to see hidden relationships between things that seemed unrelated to you just minutes ago, when you were in your more constricted state of mind. You now have access to a larger map to direct you to intuitive choices and creative solutions.

Daily Gateways to Expansion

Although any activity and situation can elicit an expansive presence, there are some that are particularly potent and offer an accelerated entry to expansion. I focus here on breathing, experiencing gratitude, expanding through language, and engaging in authentic self-expression. Other powerful gateways that I don't discuss are engaging in different forms of artistic endeavor and immersion in the transformative power of stories and myth. Finally, I've dedicated an entire chapter in Section III to Nature, which is one of the most powerful and immediate gateways to an expansive state.

Breathing

From the first breath we take when we are born to our very last breath as we leave our body, the involuntary function of breathing is readily available as a gateway to spiritual expansion. The air we breathe is what sustains us and nourishes all the cells in our body; it's what allows the human race to exist on planet Earth. As humans, we have been given life, free will, senses, and emotions to experience the world around us, and reflective and intellectual capacities to create, invent, and manifest our ideas and visions. Every breath we inhale sustains us so that we can live our full potential—individually as human beings and collectively as humanity.

Imagine that every breath you take is a gift of sacred love and support from the Universe. You are filling your body with love in the form of oxygen when you inhale, and when you exhale you are passing on this love to the plant kingdom in the form of carbon dioxide. It is a beautiful and sacred exchange of energy, of love, of creativity. If, while you are breathing, you can get a sense of the mystery and wonder of this sacred, interdependent exchange, you are bound to experience an expansive presence.

The first step is to pay attention to your breathing in order to bring your focus to the present moment. You can do that by noticing the air going in and out of your nostrils. This is a wonderful way to get your mind to stop any ongoing chatter, as it is impossible to focus on your breath while allowing thoughts to enter your mind. As soon as you are thinking, you are not focused on breathing in and breathing out. When you catch your thoughts wandering to planning or remembering, just bring your focus back to the air flowing in and out of your nostrils.

Next, you can amplify your appreciation of the present moment by visualizing the cycle of love coming into you in the form of oxygen and passing from you in the form of carbon dioxide. As you practice this, you will begin to experience the miracle of your life and the interconnectedness of reality, which will result in a spontaneous expansion of your consciousness. This is a powerful and readily available tool that you can use wherever you are, even in the presence of other people, without anyone even noticing.

You can further enhance your experience of expansiveness by noting any feeling that arises in you and acknowledging it silently, repeating, *I am feeling calm, I am feeling peaceful, I am feeling joy, I am feeling love*, etc. Allow yourself to bask in this increasing state of bliss and it will amplify your experience of expansion. Take this experience into the rest of your day, recalling this meditative moment, and you will find that you bring a fresh perspective to everything you do. This in turn will have a direct effect on all your choices, actions, and resultant outcomes.

As you do all this, you will be intentionally creating the conditions for a spiritual experience to occur on demand. This is how powerful you are. You don't have to wait for a spontaneous spiritual experience to descend upon you; you have the power to create it yourself whenever you so desire just by focusing on the miracle of your breath.

Experiencing Gratitude

The practice of gratitude offers another readily available doorway to an expansive presence. We have all experienced moments when we've counted our blessings—when we give thanks for something that happened today, appreciate a particular person in our lives, or take a moment to value something about ourselves—and when we do this, our perspective shifts and expands to a more appreciative, loving state of acceptance.

Think of something that happened to you today or in the last week for which you are grateful. Perhaps you left late for work because your child was sick, but the traffic turned out to be unusually light and you managed to arrive on time to an important meeting. During that meeting you were able to use your mediation skills to resolve a conflict that arose, and bring the meeting to a successful conclusion. That evening, reflecting back on the events of the day, you appreciate the fortunate circumstances that made that day a success when it could have turned into a disaster. Your mother-in-law helped you out with your sick child, you arrived on time in spite of having left late, and you shone when conflict threatened the outcome of the meeting.

Thinking of all this, you are filled with a sense of gratitude for the people in your life and the day's turn of events. Allow yourself to fully experience that for which you are grateful. Visualizing the situation and remembering significant details can help intensify your experience of gratitude. Note how this grateful feeling leads to a sense of expansiveness.

If you wish to amplify this expansion, try to identify additional emotional layers mixed in with this feeling of gratitude. You may become aware of an underlying feeling of joy, a sensation of warmth and calmness, or the experience of grace, to name just a few possibilities. Pay attention to any shifts in your bodily sensations and feelings so you can begin to recognize your unique way of expanding your presence. You may even notice a shift in your thought pattern and find yourself thinking, *I should stop stressing and try to keep calm, as things always seem to work out for the best.* Whatever feelings, thoughts, and sensations arise, the act of paying attention to these nuances increases your experience of gratitude and sense of expansion. As you engage in more expansive and self-caring thoughts, you will attract more favorable conditions in your daily life.

If you want to expand your consciousness through the practice of gratitude on a regular basis, you can develop the habit of counting your blessings by creating a daily written list, surrounding yourself with images or objects that remind you of your good fortune, or regularly sharing with another person how grateful you are. These practices will transform your whole attitude towards life—guaranteed!

Expanding Through Language

Language has the power to alter our consciousness. The words we speak, either out loud or as internal self-talk, evoke feelings, sensations, and entire thought patterns that are related to cultural consensus, personal memories, and underlying beliefs that inform our judgments of self and others—and they also have the power to expand or constrict our consciousness. For example, when I say to myself, *I can do this*, I am reinforcing a powerful sense of my capabilities, accompanied by a feeling of excitement and a sense of expansion. Conversely, when I say, *I can't do this*, I am emphasizing a sense of myself as limited and powerless, reinforcing a feeling of discouragement and a sense of constriction.

The more you pay attention to the language you use, the more you can influence your state of mind, which in turn will influence your entire being. As you become aware of negative self-talk and language that diminishes your self-esteem, you can consciously replace it with language that includes self-appreciation and self-empowerment. You can practice making both negative and positive statements and compare how they feel. You'll begin to identify how expansion or constriction manifests in your body. You will also gain awareness of specific feelings that are associated with an expansive or constricted state. The more you practice using statements that give you a sense of expansion, the more you will experience a life force and a vital power flowing through your entire being.

Another way to enter a state of expansive presence is to read poems that move you or meaningful quotes that uplift you. The genius of poets and writers lies in their ability to use language with accuracy and eloquence to describe aspects of human experience that resonate with something deep within us. These words stir our emotions, stimulate our intellect, and awaken our spirit, connecting us with our highest and most noble self. Thus we once again enter an expansive spiritual realm through a simple and accessible gateway.

For example, Huston Smith writes, "As human beings we are made to surpass ourselves and are truly ourselves only when transcending ourselves." The expansive language Smith uses here—"surpass" and "transcend"— reminds me of my higher aspirations. Ken Wilber's powerful quote, "Let your own presence be something that convinces the world," reminds me that fully Being in the world is more important than just Doing. When I read these quotes over and over, their meaning facilitates a shift within me, and I enter a mindful state of expansive presence, accessing my higher divine self.

Consider starting a practice of collecting quotes on your favorite subject or reading and rereading poems that most move and transport you to another plane. As you do so, pay attention to shifts in your bodily sensations, feeling states, and the thoughts that enter your mind. These are your cues. Pay attention regularly, and your level of presence and capacity for expansion will continue to grow.

Engaging in Authentic Expression

Each one of us engages in some activity that we love doing, even if it requires hard work on our part. This activity may be a hobby, a vocation, or a role we feel drawn to play—anything that evokes our passion. When we do what we love, we literally feel high and experience ourselves as a channel for something greater than our personalities and preferences. We may even feel that we are fulfilling a noble calling or our life purpose.

A businessperson may feel elated at the moment of negotiating deals; a child might feel transported when playing music; a mother could feel sheer joy when breastfeeding; and a teacher can feel immense satisfaction encountering a student's curiosity. Each person has something they love doing that transports them into an expansive state, which is often accompanied by feelings of both ease and exaltation. I feel a deep sense of conviction that opens my heart as I am writing this book.

Think of such an activity in your daily life and pay attention to how you feel when you engage in this activity. You may begin to notice that you enter an altered state. This occurs because you are engaged with something that calls you from deep within and wants to be expressed uniquely through you. Whatever the activity, whether it is your ultimate life's purpose or simply something you feel called to do at a specific moment or period in your life, when you engage in authentic expression it will evoke an immense sense of fulfillment and lead you to an expansive presence. What's more, it will likely feel like some greater force is working through you—a sure sign of expansiveness. The more you engage with what you feel called to do, the more aligned you'll be with your divine self, which will allow you to experience greater degrees of expansiveness.

Practicing an Expansive Presence

Subtle shifts in your bodily sensations, feelings, and thoughts are your guides to identifying experiences and degrees of expansion. As a modern mystic, you can study such experiences and identify the situations and conditions that bring about a sense of expansion in you. In doing so, you will develop the capacity to induce a state of expansive presence on demand.

In contrast, you can also inhibit your capacity to experience expansion through constricting sensations, emotions, and thoughts—for instance, fear, lack of trust, and rationalization.

Each person may experience expansion slightly differently and may also have various experiences at varying times. These can include a sense of elation or transcendence; a heightened experience of feelings such as joy, love, and wholeness; a profound sense of sacredness; and a quiet, peaceful recognition of truth and clarity at a given moment. I don't want to put any expectations on your experience. I am only suggesting some possibilities so that you get a sense of the potential range of experiences. Whatever you sense and feel is legitimate and appropriate for you. The more you study your own spiritual experiences and become aware of the conditions and activities that evoke this sense of vastness, the easier it will become to access and shift into a mindful, expansive presence.

Summary

- Expansive Presence involves conscious effort to identify and become more aware of spiritual experiences in your life, learning to enhance such moments and even create them intentionally and on demand.

- The sensation associated with spiritual experiences is one of expanding beyond the boundaries of your physical body.

- The overarching emotional state of spiritual experiences is one of self-love and the love of others, which can be felt and expressed in many different ways.

- Thoughts that may enter your mind while you're experiencing expansion involve a more inclusive perspective on any given situation.

- Any situation or activity can elicit a state of expansive presence with a mere shift in your perception.

- Subtle shifts in your bodily sensations, feelings, and thoughts are your guides to identifying experiences and levels of expansion.

- Certain physical, emotional, and mental activities can offer an accelerated entry into expansion:
    - Spending time in Nature
    - Engaging in any form of artistic endeavor
    - Immersion in the transformative power of stories and myth
    - Breathing
    - Experiencing gratitude
    - Expanding through language
    - Engaging in authentic self-expression.

Chapter 5

Attentive Listening:

The Key to Inner Wisdom

D o you ever make decisions based on gut feelings or intuitive hunches? Do creative ideas and solutions just pop into your head, seemingly out of nowhere? Does the world seem to rearrange itself through synchronistic events to support your specific needs?

These are examples of ordinary situations that occur to each and every one of us throughout our day. Many of us don't realize how many decisions we make based on an inner intuitive knowing. We don't perceive creative ideas as inspiring gifts from a creative Universe and pay even less attention to hidden messages from synchronistic events in our lives. Nevertheless, if you answered "yes" to any of the above questions, you have experienced the second key, Attentive Listening. This means that you have—on occasion, at least—opened yourself, intentionally or unintentionally, to a larger perception of reality and a more inclusive field of possibilities.

When your consciousness expands, it literally opens up to a larger field of awareness, which allows for a more subtle flow of information to enter your perception. A whole new world of communication with the Universe opens like a magical door, inviting you to see what was hidden from you until that moment. Whether you do this deliberately or it happens spontaneously, you begin to make new connections, and more inclusive and creative solutions enter your conscious awareness.

Access to this level of understanding is always available, but it only reveals itself when your consciousness expands. The same occurs when you switch from focused to peripheral vision. The focused vision becomes softer and wider, and you begin to see things that you were not aware of a second ago.

The key to gaining access to this wider perception is through the practice of attentive listening. The finer, more subtle realms of information that become available to you in the process can be described as intuitive guidance. It is "intuitive" because this guidance does not come from rational or deductive thinking but rather from an inner knowing that presents itself in your conscious awareness. It presents itself as "guidance" because the loving Universe is offering you a creative solution or fresh understanding of the situation on which you are focused.

Identifying Attentive Listening

Your attentive listening can focus on subtle internal experiences or on circumstantial events in the outside world. As your consciousness expands and you allow new information to enter your awareness, intuitive guidance will present itself. It may appear internally as a gut feeling or inner knowing, an intuitive flash or clear insight, a streak of creative inspiration or the sudden revelation of hidden patterns and synchronistic connections. Or it may appear externally—you may come across a book with just the message you needed to hear, or the words of a person you meet or something on the radio or TV may give you the solution to a personal concern or a problem you have encountered. External guidance and direction may also come through synchronistic encounters with animals and other natural phenomena that offer a suggestive metaphor or a new perspective on whatever currently commands your attention. Whatever the channel—internal or external—it is up to you to listen attentively and discern such guidance amid a constant flow of information.

Attentive listening requires an open, receptive presence to subtle shifts in the endless flow of information that surrounds us. It is an effortless process whereby you keep your eyes and ears open to synchronistic events and pay attention to variances in your feeling state and thought patterns.

There are four characteristics that set your specific intuitive guidance apart from your regular thoughts:

1. Intuitive guidance occurs during expansive presence, when your conscious awareness has grown to include a larger field of reality. So if you are experiencing a sense of expansion, then you can assume that the thoughts you are having and understandings you gain are of an intuitive nature.

2. Such inner knowing appears in a sudden flash, like lightning. Unlike rational thought processes, which occur as a result of logical, deductive thinking, intuitive guidance seems to materialize instantly and out of nowhere.

3. Intuitive guidance provides a full and immediate understanding of a given situation. A thought that was not there a moment ago illuminates the circumstances. This new perspective or solution is accompanied by a sense of certainty, a sudden

recognition that something is uniquely and incredibly right. It may suddenly seem like the best and only solution. Accompanying thoughts might be, *Yes, I knew that all along*, or *Why haven't I thought of that before?*

4. Intuitive guidance is accompanied by an enhanced emotional state as a result of a sudden recognition of a compelling truth. Feelings may vary from inspiration, excitement, and clarity to an opening of the heart; regardless of the feeling, intuitive guidance carries with it a sense of contentment at being connected to an inner wisdom and a higher truth.

These four attributes can help you recognize intuitive guidance and fine-tune your ability to engage in attentive listening. Always use yourself as the measurement tool, paying attention to shifts in bodily sensations, feeling states, and thought patterns that occur as you develop your capacity to receive guidance from a loving and creative Universe.

Experiences of Attentive Listening

Opportunities for attentive listening occur all the time under all sorts of circumstances. The task is to distinguish the accompanying intuitive guidance from everything else going through your head. Rather than having to rationally figure out which information is intuitive and which is logical, you need to let go and surrender, allowing the guidance to naturally enter your conscious awareness.

For example, a participant in one of my workshops had a profound insight regarding a difficult life situation through the simple act of observing the beauty of a rose. One of the exercises required participants to choose a rose from a bouquet that I had picked in my garden, to expand their consciousness by spending some time alone observing the beauty and wonder of the flower they had chosen. After some time in solitude, I asked the participants to share their experience. This deceptively simple exercise of opening up to the beauty and wonder of a flower created an expansive receptiveness in participants.

One particular woman had been dealing with a troubling family situation. She shared, "I looked at the rose and noticed an imperfection in the composition of the petals. Suddenly it hit me that rather than distracting from or marring the rose's loveliness, this imperfection is enhancing the beauty of this flower." She paused for a moment, and then with some excitement said, "I've been feeling very sad and ashamed about this family problem, but it's actually unfolding in true perfection. This seemingly imperfect rose makes me realize that."

This woman did not receive this insight through a laborious mental process but rather by surrendering to the beauty of the flower, which expanded her presence and allowed a caring message to pierce through her judgments about her life situation.

Another, perhaps more common example might involve a realization that you need to increase your income in order to make ends meet. You might not know exactly what to do, but you feel resolved to attend to this matter and change your financial situation. The minute you begin to focus on this need with resolve, the loving and creative Universe begins collaborating with you and synchronistic events start to occur. This is the principle behind the "law of attraction." Suddenly a seemingly closed door opens: an unadvertised opportunity presents itself with a higher salary and a chance for promotion. *Wow*, you think to yourself, *last week I was dreaming of such a supplement to my income, and now this comes along.* Practicing attentive listening will allow you to notice synchronistic events and stay alert to developing opportunities.

Here's a final example of using a gut feeling to make decisions: If you've ever had to choose which of several houses to buy, you know how difficult it can be to make a decision. No house is perfect or meets all of your needs, so in most cases you have to compromise. You weigh your choices and may even make a list of pros and cons for each dwelling. After a while you take some time off, as you can't seem to decide. Maybe you see a movie, take a walk, or go to sleep and have a significant dream. As you let your logical mind rest, you find yourself hearing or seeing something that helps you make a decision from a more intuitive place. Suddenly everything falls into place and your rational mind can stop trying to figure it out. You have made your choice. Your reasoning in choosing one house over another may be emotional and not factual, but it feels right. You can finally move forward with your decision.

Examples of intuitive knowing are endless because any situation can be an opportunity to receive loving guidance from a creative Universe. Practice accessing a state of expansive presence and be willing to employ attentive listening in order to receive the kind of intuitive guidance that I have described. The "trick" is to let go of your habitual reasoning and insistence on working things out for yourself and trust instead that something new and better will emerge.

Practicing Attentive Listening

In whatever form you receive intuitive guidance, the result is that some sort of knowing comes to you. A shift of perception takes place, and you feel that you now understand something that was unknown to you just moments ago. Such intuitive guidance is the reward of practicing attentive listening.

Intuitive guidance can occur spontaneously, by surprise, or intentionally. Here is a personal example of each. Both situations occurred while I was meditating.

Spontaneous Guidance

After having lived and studied in the United States I returned to Israel with my young family. After fourteen years there, it came time, for various reasons, to pack up once again and leave. My spouse wanted to move back to Northern California, where we had lived for seven years and where our first son was born, but I wanted to move to the UK and live in the community where I had experienced the spiritual awakening that led to my discovery of the Four Keys.

We decided to research schools, work opportunities, and the housing market in both the UK and California to find out which of the two places held more promise. Ultimately, California offered greater financial opportunity, although I was emotionally attached to moving to the UK. I tried to convince my spouse to settle for my preference, but he was adamant that California was the wiser choice.

I was upset that my needs were not being met, and found myself in emotional turmoil. I even neglected my meditation practice for several weeks. But finally, one morning, I decided to resume meditating. I sat down on my sofa and folded my legs beneath me, and said in my heart, "I am back. I am hurting, but I am here."

Before I had even begun to quiet my mind, I heard a clear message: "I'm trying to get you to paradise and you're fighting me."

Wow! I was stunned. These words had come in a flash, and although I didn't know who had said them, they were so powerful that I surrendered to their message without resistance. After that, I agreed to move to California. I swallowed my pride and began preparing for our move to the United States . . . and indeed it has proven to be the paradise the message I received that day promised it would be.

Intentional Guidance

I decided to go into meditation specifically for the purpose of asking the Universe for guidance on the challenges I was experiencing with writing this book. It had been a long and demanding journey—translating personal spiritual experiences into universal principles accessible to others is arduous work—and I was experiencing frustration every time I sat down to write. No matter how noble or determined my intention, I found myself trying to avoid the task of writing. So I decided to meditate on the problem and ask the Universe for guidance.

As I began meditating, I posed a question, formulating my words in silence: "Over the past decade, you have revealed to me significant insights about the nature of spiritual development. I know I need to write this book in order to get these ideas out into the world, but each time I sit down and write I feel like running away. Why have all of these ideas come through me, when you, loving and creative Universe, know that writing is so difficult for me? Couldn't you have picked an already accomplished author?"

Having finished, I sat quietly for a while—letting go of these thoughts, focusing on my breathing, clearing my mind, and enjoying a moment of emptiness and stillness. I don't know how much time passed, but after a while I felt the tingling of energy in my body which is always a sign that I am in an expanded state—a state in which the world recedes into the background and I become pure consciousness.

The initial response I got from the Universe was simple and clear: "Self-love, self-care, kindness to yourself."

I sat with that message, and as I did, more detailed guidance unfolded: "You have been given a gift and it is your duty to share it. Just as you express self-love and self-care by eating well and taking care of your body, your writing should be an act of kindness to yourself. If you write as an act of self-care, everyone will benefit; you will be self-actualizing while serving the greater good. Yes, this will demand self-discipline, but you will find your unique voice, even though it may be challenging."

As I opened my eyes I thanked the loving Universe for its clear response to my query. My entire body was alive, every part of my being fully present. I reflected on the guidance received and thought to myself, *Self-love, self-care, and kindness do not come easy. In fact, many times they are the most difficult lessons to learn. It is often easier to be kind and loving towards others than towards ourselves. But I know what it feels like to care for myself, to be gentle with myself, to be loving and non-judgmental. And so, if writing the ideas that keep coming through me is the way the Universe is offering me a lesson in self-care, then I shall have to accept the lesson with grace, and begin practicing self-love through self-expression, and kindness through writing.*

Whether you receive intuitive guidance spontaneously, just going about your day with an attitude of openness to messages from the Universe, or by intentionally asking for direction from within, you need to develop your trust in the loving intention of the creative Universe to always guide you towards the next step on your journey. By paying attention to shifts in bodily sensations, feeling states, and thought patterns, you will develop greater capacity for attentive listening and become more attuned to messages trying to get through to you. Doing so will help you differentiate intuitive guidance from deductive thinking. Once you get a taste for the magic of intuitive guidance, you will relish the relationship you develop with the loving Universe.

Summary

- When your consciousness expands, it literally opens up to a larger arena of perception, which allows for a more subtle flow of information to enter your awareness.

- Through attentive listening, a whole new world of information and communication with the Universe opens like a magical door, inviting you to see what was hidden from you until that moment.

- Attentive listening requires an open, receptive presence to subtle shifts in the endless flow of information we all receive on a daily basis.

- Attentive listening is an effortless process that requires you to keep your eyes and ears open to synchronistic events and pay attention to variances in your feeling state and thought patterns.

- The finer, more subtle realms of information that become available to you when you listen attentively can be described as intuitive guidance.

- Intuitive guidance can present itself in two ways: through subtle dimensions within you or through circumstantial events in the outside world.

- Four characteristics typify the experience of intuitive guidance:
  - Occurs during expansive presence
  - Appears in a sudden flash
  - Provides a full and immediate understanding of a given situation
  - Is accompanied by an enhanced emotional state as a result of a sudden recognition of a compelling truth.

- Intuitive guidance can occur spontaneously, or intentionally, by focusing on a specific issue, asking the Universe for guidance, and listening attentively to a response.

- By paying attention to shifts in bodily sensations, feeling states, and thought patterns during the process of attentive listening, you develop your sensitivity to intuitive guidance from the Universe.

Chapter 6

Inspired Action:

The Key to Manifesting

Have you ever experienced the satisfaction of being in the right place and doing the right thing at the right time? Have you ever acted out of inner conviction, regardless of external logic or reasoning? Have you experienced the joy that comes with having raised another person's spirit?

If you can relate to any of these situations, then you have already experienced the third key, Inspired Action. Having moved from a state of expansive presence to attentive listening, it is now time to act upon the intuitive guidance you've received and do the uniquely right thing. It is "time to act" because you have received this guidance intuitively and trust the inner knowing that has been revealed to you. Your action will be "uniquely right" because it will have the hallmark of your individual spirit and distinctive expression in the world, and yet it originates from a higher truth that is revealing itself through you.

Identifying Inspired Action

If you take the time to recall moments when you've acted out of inspiration and followed some intuitive guidance, you will recognize that, no matter how instant or matter-of-fact it might have seemed, it always involved making a choice. Therefore, the inspired action you take depends on your commitment and dedication to following through on the insight or message received.

If you were to look at inspired action through a magnifying glass, you would see that one of its components is an initial recognition that an intuitive guidance "rings true," followed by a commitment to the action it inspires. Whatever situation you may find yourself in, the two aspects of inspired action are a willingness to become a conduit for something greater to come through you and the resolve and determination to manifest it. Here's an example of how these two are expressed through inspired action.

Not so long ago, a friend shared with me a difficult decision he made to promote a long-overdue healing. Thirty years had passed since he and his ex-wife had gone through a bitter divorce, and in all that time, he had not spoken with her as he found the gulf between them too great to breach. What prompted this desire to reconnect was a journey to the East Coast for a school reunion, where he happened to pass the house where they had lived in the earliest stage of their marriage. He was overcome with nostalgia and a sense of loss. In that moment his heart opened, expanding his awareness beyond the stale perspective from which he had viewed their marriage for so long. He had a sudden inner prompting that translated as, "It is time to heal this old quarrel."

This message was followed by an understanding that the right thing to do would be to contact his ex-wife and resume some sort of communication. He and his ex were now well up in years, and he did not want to exit his life with this old hurt still festering. Although the thought of contacting her was painful for him, he surrendered to this deep inner knowing that would not go away. Overcoming his resistance, he summoned his will and made the difficult phone call to reconnect.

My friend had to reinforce this will to act over and over again in the year that followed, as it took many meetings for him and his ex-wife to progress in the desired healing. Each time the resistance resurrected itself, it had to be replaced with an expansive sense of this being the right thing to do. Every few months they met for a lunch or dinner and examined the old pain, each taking responsibility for their role in what had happened—and ultimately, with persistence from both of them, a significant healing occurred that greatly improved their relationship.

This example of inspired action is highly emotionally charged, but not all inspired actions are. In fact, we each encounter on a daily basis plenty of ordinary, less fraught situations where we perceive some intuitive guidance that requires our inspired action.

Experiences of Inspired Action

I have identified five types of inspired action that you might encounter in the regular course of your day. Each type has a distinct essence, and yet they all share the underlying qualities of expansiveness, the willingness to surrender to a greater truth, and an impulse to action.

In the Flow

This type of inspired action feels like every traffic light turns green just as you approach it. It feels like the Universe is supporting you in everything you do. But it requires attentive listening to your inner promptings.

Rachel, one of the women who participated in my doctoral study, shared in our first interview a story that illustrates this type of inspired action:

"I was out driving this morning and there was this amazing rainbow, that black, black storm on one side and a rainbow on the other side; and then there was this gas station and something in me said, 'Stop now, stop at this gas station,' even though I never stop in this specific gas station. So I stopped and put air in my tire, and when I did I noticed it had a screw stuck in it. I knew I was ten minutes from a flat tire. So, I had to deal with this puncture, and there just happened to be a puncture repair service at this station. I just said, 'Oh, my gosh, what are the odds?' because there's never a puncture service in a gas station. Ten dollars' worth of damage versus a blown tire on the highway, in the rain . . . Then you're waiting for the tow, you tow the car, replace the tire . . . It was such a great feeling and I can give myself credit because it wasn't cognitive, it was an instinct. It was all triggered by the rainbow, an outside force of God, of nature. There's no connection between a rainbow and the decision I made, impromptu, to pull off the road. It's absurd, of course. It's ridiculous, not intellectually logical, but some force out there is smiling on me today. So I'm happy saying it was a spiritual thing and if that's absurd to some people, it doesn't matter to me."

Against All Odds

Sometimes the action you are inspired to take seems to run counter to many reasonable voices around you, or even within yourself; though it goes against all odds, you know it's something you must do.

This type of inspired action is different than stubbornly banging your head against the wall and insisting on doing it "your way" when saner voices around you counsel otherwise. Discerning between an inner spiritual knowing and just being stubborn is a delicate process, but we each have it in us to figure it out.

One way to distinguish between stubbornness and inner knowing is to notice whether you are acting out of fear and a need to control the outcome of a situation, or if your motivation seems to be coming from an intuitive, expansive, and inspired presence.

Karen, another participant in my study, shared a story about following her inner conviction against all outside advice and logical arguments. Her life had taken a dramatic change: she had lost her spouse and was now a single mom, raising two small children, ages two and four. She decided to relocate from South Africa to Israel—leaving behind her extended support system and uprooting her family—based on what she called "a knowingness." Here is how she recounted the story in our interview:

"When I made my decision to make Aliya (immigration to Israel), I'm not sure what it was, but for some reason in that point in my life there was no doubt in my mind. My car was stolen, and the police came, and I was so calm. They said, 'We've never seen anyone so calm.' And my thought was, *Now I don't have to sell it! This is perfect!* There was just this deep, deep trusting . . . it felt very spiritual. I felt very connected, so that in the process nothing deterred me, nothing made me think that it's not the right thing to do. Somehow I think I'm just meant to be here [in Israel]. Everyone told me, particularly Israelis, 'You'll never manage; it's so hard.' My family was saying, 'What do you need to go for?' I had no money; I had these two little babies, all on my own. But I just knew that this is my path. It was not logical . . . there was a knowingness."

Changing Your Attitude

Another type of inspired action involves changing your attitude towards any given situation and, by doing so, changing the experience and the perceived outcome from what at first seemed negative to one that feels positive. A boring chore can suddenly turn into something that inspires gratitude and contentment, or a challenging period in your life can become a significant and fulfilling opportunity for growth and transformation.

A participant in one of my workshops shared how she often turns a tedious chore into a moment of grateful reflection. "When I fold my laundry, it is not the most exciting task but I turn it into something different. I count my blessings and don't think how unexciting the task is, but how I could be so much worse off, recognizing that my life is good, my children are happy, and I have a job I love."

I recall such a reframe of my own attitude making a tremendous difference in my life. I spoke in Chapter 2 about my childhood with an alcoholic mother. This was a very difficult situation that understandably left many scars. But as I grew into adulthood, I kept acting like a righteous victim, feeling that my mother had destroyed my life forever. It was only when I got into recovery as a child of an alcoholic that I moved from victimhood to self-empowerment, embracing a path towards self-realization and service to the conscious awakening of others. I was able to reframe the difficulties of my childhood and see them as a gift—an opportunity for my soul to grow, and for me to become a more compassionate and whole human being.

This kind of shift in attitude, even years after the fact, can change the meaning of any situation to something more life-affirming. We each have the choice to see the silver lining in every cloud. You have the capacity to change your interpretation of any event and, by doing so, change the moral of the stories you tell yourself. This allows you to come out the other side with a more inspiring perspective. Your life situation might not have changed, but your focus has shifted to the blessing within the situation, which makes all the difference. As you begin to consistently change your attitude towards everything that happens, you will find that you are blessed with more daily miracles and magical synchronicities, and a life that runs more smoothly and harmoniously.

Practice Makes Perfect

This type of inspired action is intentional and involves choosing to focus on a specific quality throughout the day. Any sensation, feeling, or thought can qualify as a quality to work with. For example, you could choose to practice experiencing a sense of peace throughout the day, a feeling of joy, or a thought such as, *I enjoy being loved and cared for by the Universe.* Whatever you choose, create the intention to practice this feeling or thought and then observe how it presents itself to you as you go about your day.

Let's say you choose to connect to the beauty all around you. You create an intention, asking for beauty to be revealed to you. You might form a sentence that you repeat throughout the day, and mark the connection with people you meet by saying in your heart, "I see your inner beauty." If you create the intention to see beauty during your day, the Universe will reveal to you many moments of beauty. Perhaps your attention will be drawn to a small leaf that lands next to your feet during a lunch break in the park, and you may find yourself lingering over its unique colors and form. You may notice that a colleague does an especially eloquent and graceful job presenting to your clients; you may go to the movies that evening and pay special attention to the aesthetics of the film. Taking the time to enjoy these moments is part of the practice of inviting beauty into your life.

Pay attention to shifts in sensations, feelings, and thoughts as you practice this type of inspired action. As you connect to your spiritual essence through this simple yet profound practice you will begin to expand your consciousness, leading to feelings of elation and bliss. This is a powerful way to change your outlook on life and become aware of your true nature. It will help you see the perfection of everything within and around you.

Raising Someone's Spirit

The final type of inspired action I address involves the power we have to change and expand the consciousness of others around us. We not only have the capacity to uplift ourselves, we also have the capacity to raise the spirits of people we encounter.

I am sure you have had the experience of standing in line at the supermarket or at the bank, and the cashier does not look very happy. You consciously decide to say a kind word and it brings a smile to his face. At that moment, you have taken an action that changes the state of mind of that person. Suddenly, their spirit is uplifted. For a moment you have seen them more positively than they were experiencing themselves.

We have the power to see each other through caring eyes and offer another person an uplifting perspective that expands their perception of themselves. It is a choice we make at every moment, a choice to plant seeds of love, care, joy, and inspiration wherever we go. It can open up opportunities for soulful encounters with strangers and can be the trigger for your day running more smoothly and everything working out perfectly. So pay attention to opportunities that present themselves and require your intuitive engagement.

Practicing Inspired Action

Following through on intuitive guidance with an inspired action is a practice that is bound to create a qualitative shift in your life. When you practice inspired action, you will find that the loving, creative Universe will reveal itself to you in magical and wondrous ways, and you will recognize with greater frequency the occurrence of miracles and synchronistic events in your life.

I perceived the kind of magic I'm referring to in a very ordinary situation. One time, when I was working with my team in the living room of my house, my son came into the room and the two of us began a conversation that

I soon realized was going to escalate into an argument. At the time, I had been practicing the Four Keys for a few years and had gotten to a place where I was always on the alert, sensitive to signs that the Universe was communicating with me. In this incidence, I was about to react to my son in an authoritative parental manner, which would no doubt have worsened the situation, when my attention was suddenly diverted by a most unusual sight: outside the window, the trees expanded backwards for maybe five seconds, and then returned to their regular position.

This was clearly not merely the wind blowing through the trees, and I couldn't believe what I was seeing; it was like a special effect in a movie, something that was not physically possible. It was striking enough to stop me in my tracks—giving me the chance to recompose myself and realize that I needed to stop the argument with my son and find an elegant way to disengage. I interpreted the momentary expansion I saw in the trees as a suggestion that I, too, expand my perspective. I shifted my approach from authoritarian to egalitarian, which allowed both me and my son to let go of the positions we were holding and defuse the situation.

I returned to my team meeting feeling both appreciative of the quick shift in the outcome of the situation and astounded by the vision that had instigated this shift.

Engaging regularly in inspired actions will change the way you interact with the world; you will become a creative influence on your surroundings, and your appreciation of how events unfold around you will be enhanced. The miraculous, hidden within the ordinary, will become more readily apparent, and your experience of awe more frequent. Your impact in the world will become more powerful and result in more positive outcomes. You will feel truly blessed.

Summary

- Inspired action occurs when you listen to both inner and outer promptings and choose to act upon their intuitive guidance.

- The overarching characteristics of inspired action are a willingness to become a conduit for something greater and a resolve and determination to manifest it.

- Types of inspired actions you might encounter in the course of your day include:

  - *In the flow*—Feels like the Universe is supporting you and everything seems to fall into place at the right time

  - *Against all odds*—Acting out of inner conviction despite external logic or counsel

  - *Changing your attitude*—Altering your approach to any given situation and, by doing so, changing the experience of what at first seemed negative into something positive

- ***Practice makes perfect***—Intentionally focusing on and expressing a specific feeling or quality throughout your day

- ***Raising someone's spirit***—Purposefully contributing to the uplifting of another person's attitude.

- Following through on intuitive guidance with inspired action will increase the frequency of miracles and synchronistic events in your life, revealing the magical and wondrous ways in which the loving and creative Universe can manifest itself.

Chapter 7

Faith-Filled Knowing:

The Key to Ongoing Co-Creation

H as listening to your intuition increased your confidence in a loving and creative Universe as a guiding force in your life? Has experiencing synchronistic events strengthened your faith in the existence of a spiritual reality? Have you ever found that a painful and challenging experience actually occurred at the perfect time and was significant to your personal growth?

If any of these experiences feel familiar to you, then you have already encountered the fourth key, Faith-Filled

Knowing. This final key develops through a gradual realization that, just as certain laws underlie the physical world, there are also principles that govern the spiritual realm. When we live a conscious, spiritually guided, and materially grounded life, these spiritual laws begin manifesting through daily signs, miracles, and synchronicities that strengthen our faith in the existence of a spiritual reality directly affecting our material existence.

Carl Jung was asked in an interview for the BBC in 1959 whether or not he had believed in God as a child, to which he responded, "Oh, yes." He was then asked whether or not he believed in God now that he was eighty-four years old. After some thought, Jung answered, "Now?" Long pause. "Difficult to answer. I know. I do not need to believe. I know."

What Jung spoke of was faith-filled knowing, the inner conviction that there is a divine and sacred dimension, and that we humans are a beloved part of this reality. This knowing is not an intellectual understanding but a very personal experience of perceiving and participating in a spiritual existence. This kind of knowing comes from ongoing experiences that confirm the existence of a transcendent spirit and its manifestation in our very real physical world.

Using our intuitive inner guidance we can develop an intimate and co-creative relationship with different aspects of this spiritual reality, allowing for different principles to manifest on our earthly plane. It is a relationship of cooperation because we receive guidance on how to live our daily life in alignment with our purpose, calling, and destiny, and in return we become an expression and material manifestation of this spiritual plane.

Identifying Faith-Filled Knowing

A child learns to walk through reinforcement. First, she begins by wobbling forward with the help of an adult who holds her hands to steady her. You often see children begging their parents to help them walk again and again at this age; that's positive reinforcement, which leads to a determination to continue.

Next, the child crawls towards a table, picks herself up, and walks while holding on to the edge. That action gives her a positive reward of achievement and a newly discovered freedom.

The "table walk" mastered, the child next ventures out and tries to let go, taking a step into the unknown without a safety net. And she may fall on her bum at first—but if she does, she picks herself up with the help of the table and tries again. This is still positive reinforcement, although it can be frustrating at times to keep falling and having to try again.

At some point, the child will take one step without any support, and if her head happens to hit the table on her way down, she will cry out as she lands on the floor. This hurts and is even a little scary; nevertheless, most children will get back to it within minutes, trying again and again until they learn to walk.

While hitting her head on the table can be perceived as a negative experience, you could argue that all the feedback this toddler received from her varying attempts to walk was positive, as every attempt furthered her mission to experience the world vertically.

The same occurs as we develop our faith-filled knowing. Some experiences are a positive reinforcement that a loving Universe exists and is guiding our every step; others are challenging experiences with a perceived negative outcome, and yet they, too, further us on our journey towards self-realization and wholeness.

Experiences that offer positive reinforcement occur when we feel we are in the flow and everything is going our way. For example, perhaps you have a hunch that it is time to sell your house and you follow through on it. The real estate market plummets right after you sell, and you feel relieved and appreciative that you followed your instinct. Or maybe you leave your mobile phone on during a meeting, which you never usually do, and ten minutes in you receive a call that your child is sick and needs to be picked up from school. Or you could listen to an inner prompting to make a career change and go back to school, which leads you to discovering your life's purpose. Experiences like these tend to reinforce reliance on your intuition and strengthen your belief in being constantly guided by some force that is coaxing you towards greater freedom, happiness, and fulfillment.

Challenging experiences with a perceived negative outcome can be much harder to see as stepping-stones to a more enlightened existence. In retrospect, though, you may come to understand such trying times as having been integral to your personal or professional growth, difficult as it may be to view them as such in the moment.

As I mentioned earlier, I felt like a victim of my mother's alcoholism for many years; eventually, however, I arrived at a moment in my adult life where I actually experienced genuine gratitude towards my mom for creating the circumstances that led me into a twelve-step program, and for the rich emotional and spiritual experiences that followed. Another example could be having to close down a business you've invested years in, and experiencing it as one of the most trying times of your life, only to discover that this experience leads you to find your authentic life calling. Or a relationship that you thought would last forever ends abruptly, leaving you depressed for months, but eventually you begin dating again and find the person who is really right for you.

Such experiences are challenging for a period of time, but if we learn from them and become stronger and more complete human beings as a result, they turn into significant milestones on our journey towards greater personal and professional freedom. If you adopt the approach that you can learn something from everything that happens to you, you can develop your faith from every experience, both the positive and the seemingly negative.

Examples of Faith-Filled Knowing

Faith-filled knowing usually develops over time through repeatedly acting upon inner promptings. However, we may occasionally experience a more dramatic event that provides a quantum leap in our perspective, propelling us from believing in a spiritual reality to knowing it exists.

The following two stories illustrate how both a positive and a seemingly negative experience can strengthen our faith-filled knowing.

Sharon's Story

Sharon was one of the women in the study that I conducted for my doctoral dissertation on the Four Keys. The study consisted of two groups: one that met regularly over the course of a year and another that met only four times.

As Sharon was part of the latter group, it was essential that she participate in all four sessions—but in the first session I took the group outside to engage with an exercise in nature, and Sharon's hay fever limited her participation. During the second session she had an allergic reaction to the four cats in my house and had to leave halfway through. She attended the third session, but before the fourth session took place she was diagnosed with myocarditis, an infection of the heart muscle, and she couldn't attend our final meeting. It turned out that all her allergic symptoms were related to her dangerous heart condition.

As she had missed significant portions of the program, it seemed doubtful that Sharon would have accumulated enough experiences to contribute to the study. But on the same morning that the rest of us were meeting for our fourth and final session, Sharon had a profound spiritual experience that made her overall experience significant to the study.

Sharon had just gone through a particularly stressful year; besides her own health problems, her daughter had undergone several operations due to a problem in her head and spine. On the morning of the final session of the study group, Sharon left a message on my mobile phone, sending us all loving thoughts, and we said a prayer for her quick recovery.

While we were meeting, Sharon was resting at home. At some point, she went out onto her terrace and began reading the newspaper. Something she read reminded her of the prayer her mother used to chant when lighting the Sabbath candles. Sharon began singing that song, remembering the sweet voice of her mother, who had passed away thirty years earlier, and suddenly she felt the presence of her mother enveloping her. The presence was so strong that she actually felt her mother was there, holding and comforting her. She told me later that she had not had such a visceral experience of her mom since her death.

"You know that I am with you, right?" her mother said. "You are not alone."

A warm feeling of love washed through Sharon, and she responded, "Yes, I know you are with me."

Her mom stayed with her for a moment and then disappeared, but for the rest of the day, Sharon was in an altered state, basking in the warm glow of her mother's love. For Sharon, this was a much-needed and uplifting reassurance. For the rest of us, it confirmed the undeniable existence of a spiritual plane and reinforced our faith-filled knowing.

Returning to our metaphor of the child learning to walk, this is an example of developing a capacity through positive reinforcement. An experience such as the one Sharon had with her mom is so powerfully undeniable that it reinforces our faith-filled knowing, making it easy to believe in the existence of a spiritual plane.

A Relative Passes Away

A few years ago, a relative of mine passed away. While I had never been particularly close to him, his spouse and I shared a loving connection, and I wanted to extend my support. As I was living in a different country, I wondered what might be the best way to help.

A few days before the funeral I had a profound

spiritual experience, similar to Sharon's, where I too felt washed with love by the sudden presence of someone I recognized as my departed relative. I can't explain how I knew it; I just had this deep inner knowing that his presence was near.

He had suffered from Alzheimer's for nearly a decade before passing away, so he had not been able to communicate directly with his family for some time. As I relaxed into the warm feeling of love enveloping me, I heard him internally urging me to share a message in his name:

> *Life seems long when looking forward, but short when looking backwards. While still alive, you have a chance to change your ways. Let go of old quarrels and express your love to those you care for the most. Please pass this message on to my loved ones.*

This was a powerful message, and I wondered what would be the best way to convey it to my relatives, who were so far away. I was concerned they might think it odd and was hesitant to share my unusual experience. But I felt a sacred duty to pass on the message with which I had been entrusted, so I decided to write a letter and have someone read it at the funeral on my behalf.

The response to my letter took me by surprise. The deceased's spouse got upset with me. "He wasn't capable of expressing such messages," she said. "I've been taking care of him for almost a decade and I haven't been able to communicate with him at all. He's been like a little child. So don't come to me now that he's gone with some profound message that you claim he communicated to you."

While I was taken aback by her response, I interpreted it as a momentary release of anger after so many hard years of taking care of an ill spouse. But she didn't stop there; she kept sending me angry letters. I lessened all contact for a while.

This was very upsetting, as we'd always had a special connection and cared for each other very much. I even regretted having written the letter, as its purpose had been so misinterpreted. Her inability to let go of this incident and move on confirmed why my deceased relative had contacted me in the first place.

After months of wrestling with myself, I concluded that I had been presented with this experience for two reasons: to pass on a much-needed message to the deceased's spouse and to strengthen my faith-filled knowing in spite of a seemingly negative consequence. Once I reframed the negative incident, my perception shifted and helped reinforce my belief in a spiritual reality.

Practicing Faith-Filled Knowing

Practicing the Four Keys is the way to develop your faith in a spiritual existence and integrating its wisdom into your daily material living. The more you consciously participate in cycles of expansion, guidance, and action, the more you will be able to perceive spiritual laws manifesting in your life. This in turn will strengthen your faith in a spiritual reality. Through the repeated practice of these Four Keys, you will develop a deep inner knowing that you are in a cooperative relationship with the hidden intelligence of the Universe, with a loving Universe, and that you have a unique role to play in the web of life.

Summary

- Faith-Filled Knowing is the realization and inner conviction that there is a divine and sacred force in the Universe, of which we humans are a beloved part.

- An experience of transcendence and the feeling of being in union with a larger spiritual reality are the hallmarks of faith-filled knowing.

- Developing your faith is not an intellectual understanding but a very personal experience of perceiving and participating in a spiritual reality.

- Faith-filled knowing comes from experiences that confirm the existence of a loving and creative Universe and its manifestation in our very real physical world.

- You can strengthen your faith by engaging in an ongoing cooperative relationship with the Universe through the use of the Four Keys.

Section III

Accelerating Your
Spiritual Development

Chapter 8

The Four Keys Come Together

Not so long ago, I was under financial stress. We had moved to the US from Israel a year before, and only my husband had gotten a work permit. For quite a few months we had very little money and anxiously awaited each bi-monthly paycheck. We comforted each other and tried to be reassuring and upbeat about it, but the stress got to us. One morning the dire realization came full upon me: *The balance in the account is six dollars and we have no savings. When what I am eating now is gone, I will not be able to buy any more. If I drive my car and run out of gas, I can drive no further.*

Most of us, I'm sure, have experienced at some time some degree of stress around finances. Well, we had come to our "bottom."

I remember standing in the kitchen thinking these thoughts as I was looking out the window into the garden, where there is a fountain with water running down a sphere. A few birds usually come visit that fountain every day, and it is always beautiful to see them. This particular morning, the fountain was attracting more and more birds. There were at least fifteen of them, all with different colors and markings. Some alighted on the fountain's edge, others hovered in the air around it, back and forth, in and out. It was glorious!

As I was watching this parade of birds, enjoying the small, delicate beauty of each of them, I wondered who had bestowed such variety upon them: the glossy black eyeliner, the iridescent chest, the gray, green, or bright scarlet head, feather patterns of light and dark, the streaky and vivid shoulder patches. Lost in my admiration, I was filled with gratitude for the abundance that paraded before me, rich in color, size, and detectable individual character. Suddenly I felt I did not lack anything. With all of this beauty right in front of my eyes, I had so much abundance.

A thought entered my mind: "I should count my blessings. I have a house; I have shelter; I have food; I have heat in my house; I have a car outside; I have a spouse whom I love and who loves me; I have two wonderful children, both in wonderful schools that nourish their intellect and spirit; I have immediate and extended family whom I love, dear friends where I live and in other parts of the world." I felt surrounded by an available love I could call upon in any moment of need, and I even had six dollars in my bank account after having paid for my kids' schools and the car, after the rent, the food, and the heat.

Counting my blessings, I was able to shift from a perspective of scarcity to one of abundance. My perception of the same situation, having a total of six dollars "to my name," had been transformed from a suffering of lack to thankfulness for plenty. Abundance is not about how much money is in my bank account, I realized, but how blessed I am.

Within a few days, an unexpected refund came in the mail and helped see us through until the next paycheck. Since that powerful incident, each time financial stress has loomed I've remembered that the loving Universe is abundant, and I've trusted it to guide me to a creative, and often miraculous, solution.

Living the Four Keys

Just before I looked out the window and saw the birds, my attention was primarily focused on how we would survive till our next paycheck, and I could feel myself contracting with fear. But seeing the unusually large congregation around the fountain outside my window made me snap out of my worries. The beauty and playful ease of the birds drew me in. My focus expanded from a narrow one of fear to a seemingly boundless sense of wonder. I had been taken into the first key, a sense of Expansive Presence. I was open and receptive to the different ways in which the Universe invites us to expand our consciousness.

Once in this expansive state, I became spontaneously receptive to the second key, Attentive Listening, and heard an intuitive guidance to count my blessings. This suggestion, to which I had but moments before been oblivious, was not a logical, deductive thought. Instead, it entered my conscious awareness out of nowhere, inviting me to follow its guidance. What gave it an "aha" power was the fact that it was accompanied by a unique sense of being right—that "ring of truth" I mentioned in an earlier chapter.

Having heard clearly this message, I made the conscious choice to move into the third key, Inspired Action. I began to count my blessings, which felt uplifting and helped me gain an expanded perspective on my financial situation. In a very short time I went from lamenting what I perceived as lack in my life to feeling thankful for the blessings I now perceived were so abundantly bestowed upon me. As I listed each blessing in my life, I was filled with gratitude at their number and potency.

After I finished counting, I felt liberated, and a sense of elation came over me. Aware of the Four Keys being at

play, I attentively opened myself up to yet another intuitive inspiration and followed through on it. I continued
to count my blessings every day until I could truly experience the ongoing abundance in my life.

Regardless of your level of awareness, inspired action
always requires a conscious decision to act upon the
intuitive guidance. The more you practice using the Four
Keys in your daily life, the more confidence you will gain
to act in inspired ways.

I recognized that the radical shift in my perspective
on scarcity and abundance had not happened on its own
but rather by an invisible guidance that had revealed to
me the interconnectedness of life. This was a moment
of Faith-Filled Knowing. With the help of the birds, I
entered a field of consciousness where I tapped into the
innate intelligence of the Universe and gained access to
a higher wisdom regarding scarcity and abundance. I was
propelled towards a new perspective, one far more positive and useful than the crippling one I had been caught
up in before the bird incident.

The abundance of birds, a much greater number than
usual and so varied in markings and colors and activity,
seemed to "say" to me, "You are just as abundant in blessings as these birds." This instant, transcendent realization
reinforced my faith in the interdependent and co-creative
dance between the loving Universe, nature, and myself.

This kind of faith-filled knowing will not always
make sense to your rational mind. Instead, it may seem

like a sudden leap, a sudden certitude that there is a hidden force guiding you. Trust this inner knowing and it will strengthen your faith in the spiritual nature of reality, which in turn will allow you to experience the Four Keys more intensely and regularly throughout your day.

The Grace of a Spiritual Perspective

The incident with the birds turned out to be a spontaneous spiritual experience. I did not intentionally change my perspective from one of worry to one of contentment, and I was not seeking guidance. However, having adopted the Four Keys as my primary framework for perceiving and interpreting my experiences, I quickly realized that the prompting to count my blessings was intuitive guidance presenting itself to me. This allowed me to participate more fully in this wondrous collaboration with the Universe and to surrender to the magic of the moment.

Most of us are unaware of the continuous spiritual experiences that occur in our daily lives. You might feel a sense of elation during a productive and creative work session but not recognize it as a moment of expansive presence; you might make decisions based on your intuition and appreciate how "spot-on" you can be but fail to realize that these are attentive listening and inspired action at play.

Practicing the Four Keys can help you perceive with greater ease this pervasive spiritual dimension in your daily life. When you open up and allow yourself to be transported to a state of grace, you transcend your ordinary, habitual, and all-too-often limited state of mind—and in turn, a gateway to the Universe opens, showering you with love, guidance, and daily miracles. All that remains for you to do is to stay engaged in this co-creative dance, imbuing your relationships, choices, and expression in the world with an uplifting and life-affirming spiritual perspective.

Chapter 9

Dedicating Yourself to Practicing the Four Keys

As is the case with any goal you set, you need to dedicate yourself to the path that will bring you the tangible results you seek. The same is true with working with the Four Keys. In order to achieve evident results, you need to apply the Four Keys consistently, so that you can experience the self-improvement you seek. There are five commitments that can ground your spiritual development and help you get the most out of practicing these Keys.

Commitment #1: Make a Conscious Choice

Don't drift through life letting the world thrash you around in the hope that good things will just come knocking on your door. It is not enough to simply brace yourself until the bad things go away. You have to make a conscious choice to participate in the design of your life and put in the work it takes to bring about good things. You have to want to better your situation and make a deliberate decision to do what it takes to make it happen. This doesn't mean you need to do it by your will alone; on the contrary, you need to create the intention and then ask the loving Universe to support and guide you so that it feels like a co-creative dance.

The Four Keys can help you do that with greater ease. But you need to choose to practice expanding your awareness, whether through conscious breathing, the practice of gratitude, authentic expression, or any other accessible gateway. It is essential that you train yourself to listen attentively to intuitive guidance and summon the courage to act upon this guidance and give life to what is asking to come through you. Otherwise, you will continue having random moments of elation and inspiration but will not be able to fully express your unique spiritual essence in your everyday life.

When I was shown the doorway to the hidden world that I had longed for since the moment of my birth, I committed to becoming proficient in walking back and forth between the two worlds: our material earthly existence and the seemingly hidden spiritual reality. When the Four Keys were revealed to me, I found that they could serve as an accessible and readily available road-map to elevating my daily existence and bringing spirituality down to earth. But it took a burning desire, and a lot of perseverance, to transcend my daily existence and become skillful at doing it. Know that you have the power to choose, as well as the tools to elevate your daily existence; now you just have to use them in order to live a spiritually fulfilling and materially satisfying life.

Commitment #2: Show Up Fully

Now that you've made the decision to practice the Four Keys, it is time to show up fully and engage in a co-creative partnership with the Divine, Spirit, the Source, the Universe, or whatever you choose to call this spiritual reality. While this may sound like an intangible connection, it is not merely a metaphor; it is a concrete partnership that will yield concrete results. In this collaborative relationship, you need to show up 100 percent, doing your part. Only then can a loving and creative Universe fully offer itself back to you.

You can choose to give your attention to any area of your life—your health, wealth, relationships, expression in the world, or spiritual development—and you can choose to focus on any specific issue within one of these areas. Whatever you choose, there are a few things you can do to play your part in this co-creative dance. First, practice living in a state of expansive presence so that you can hear, see, perceive, and intuit when the Universe is communicating with you. Second, ask the loving Universe for help and guidance and notice how it is directing your decisions and actions through daily miracles and synchronistic events. Third, engage in inspired action that will move you forward in your aspirations, help resolve challenges, create more wholeness in your life, and contribute to your unique expression in the world.

Commitment #3: Face Challenges

Practicing the Four Keys gives you tools to deal with life's challenges, but it will not eliminate them completely. You are bound to face different struggles throughout your life: conflicts with family and friends, endless professional demands, and internal turmoil. The difficulties you encounter and the trials you will have to overcome are an integral part of living, but as you establish a more spiritual approach to your life and live in greater alignment with the Universe and your unique place within it, life will begin to run more smoothly, with miracles and synchronistic events supporting you along the way.

Without a spiritual perspective, you may feel like a victim of circumstances when you come up against challenges. Adopting a spiritual perspective can provide a renewed understanding of a given situation, offer a lesson that needs to be learned, and help you grow and become a more whole, compassionate, and wise human being. Such benefits will require you to release limiting beliefs and change habitual behaviors that hold you back from becoming the clear and fine-tuned vessel necessary to manifest your full and unique being.

Specific challenges are bound to arise when engaging in spiritual growth. The many derivatives of fear and narrow-mindedness hinder you from accessing and developing your full spiritual being. Doubting your capacity to be highly intuitive, over-rationalizing and dismissing synchronistic events, or judging intuitive guidance that defies logic are frequent challenges that will constrict your consciousness rather than expand it. Some of us live in perpetual self-doubt, while others over-rationalize. Which form of fear and narrow-mindedness undermines your own inherent spiritual nature? Practicing the first key of expansive presence can help you face and manage your doubts and fears, moving you to a constructive mindset of love, care, and endless possibilities.

Commitment #4: Examine Your Self-Worth

One of the most important questions to ask yourself as you practice the Four Keys is whether you are worthy of an ongoing, intimate relationship with a loving and creative Universe. After all, that implies that you are deserving of special attention on a daily basis. In our troubled world, does some higher power have the time to specifically guide you towards manifesting your full potential and calling in this lifetime? Does the creative force in the Universe really perceive "little" you as a precious, integral strand in the web of life and therefore a vital contributor to the overall well-being of the whole of existence?

A woman in one of my workshops who had strong ethics and values regarding social justice felt that many other people in the world merited more ongoing guidance from Spirit than she did. She felt that others were more deserving or more in need than she was, and that she could "wait her turn." This may seem noble or unselfish of her, but it also speaks of a deep sense of unworthiness. She was caught in a dualistic, either/or mindset where there is not enough to go around. Being kind and generous in nature, she was willing to forgo her birthright and need for an intimate relationship with a loving Universe. She could not conceive of herself as an equally essential part of an interrelated web of the whole of existence.

While your initial response to whether you are worthy of this sacred relationship with a loving Universe may seem like an obvious "yes," it may take you some time to really take in the magnitude of the implications of such a relationship. It is an ongoing process of recognizing and surrendering to the reality that you are an indispensable point of consciousness in the Universe and are truly loved and cared for, regardless of your fortune. This may require a radical shift of perspective on your part. As you peel off the layers that obscure your perception, you will open yourself up to the miracle of life and experience the true wonder of your existence.

Commitment #5: Find Your Divine Purpose

Find out what you love doing and what you do well, what inspires and motivates you, and what nourishes and fulfills you. That is your compass to finding your divine purpose.

You might have a clear vocation in mind; perhaps you feel that your life calling is to contribute to a specific field, like being a teacher or a musician, or you may aspire to contribute your leadership or coordinating skills to the greater good of an organization. Both of these paths require an innate gift that you possess or develop through experience, such as an ear for melody and rhythm, a talent for communicating ideas and inspiring others, or a gift for attending to the many details that go into managing a project.

A different kind of divine purpose may fall under the less tangible category of "aspirations." You might be a person who is inspired to uplift the environment or emotional sphere in which you live and move, feeling that your life calling is to spread love and compassion wherever you go. While your exact vocation might be less obvious, you may be able to share your mission in a wide variety of settings, and with anyone and everyone you encounter.

My divine purpose falls under the latter category; it

is to live an abundant life of service. I do this with sacred intention—as a mother to my two sons, a co-creator with my life partner, a support to my friends around the world, and, hopefully, a vehicle of transformation through this book.

What is your divine purpose? Whether you are still searching or have already found your life's mission, use the Four Keys to receive concrete answers as to how to move forward. "Ask and you shall receive." The Universe is waiting to collaborate with you.

Moving Forward

Applying the five commitments will propel you forward on your spiritual journey. By *making a conscious choice* to practice the Four Keys, you will enhance your capacity to perceive and appreciate daily miracles. When you commit to *showing up fully*, you will experience your power to make a difference in your world. *Facing challenges* as they present themselves will help you grow and reveal opportunities to heal parts of yourself that long to be made whole. *Examining your self-worth* will open you up to the sacredness and preciousness of your life and everything around you. And *finding your divine purpose* will show you the way to express your special role in the dance of life, propelling you to become your best self and serving the world in your own unique way.

Chapter 10

Finding Wholeness Through
Unity in Nature

A few years ago I visited a friend in the English countryside during the summer. She lived in a farmhouse
surrounded by fields with high grass and wildflowers. One
morning, just after waking up, I lay in bed looking out
through the large window at the beautiful rolling hills,
admiring their dark green trees and bright green pastures.
I felt so grateful to be able to witness this spectacular view
just by raising my head and was in awe of the beauty that
lay before me. My heart overflowed with joy.

Suddenly, I had this clear understanding that seemed to come from nowhere and yet resonated as true, leaving no doubt: "Nature is in perfect balance between its physical attributes and its spiritual qualities; it is a manifestation of the unity of spirit and matter." The rolling hills and green pastures had clear physical form, each tree and plant its own distinct shape and hue. Yet it also emanated metaphysical, spiritual qualities that I could access as I looked out through the window—an overall sense of expansiveness that was expressed through beauty, peacefulness, grandeur, patience, and delight.

Except for when we humans interfere through different forms of pollution, nature always maintains this unity between its physical attributes and spiritual properties. When we spend time in nature, this sense of expansiveness rubs off on us and we experience greater unity and harmony of mind, body, and spirit.

When our actions are aligned with our spiritual essence, we humans are capable of experiencing that same balance. When we reach that level of harmony, we derive joy and pleasure from the work we do in the world; we feel highly energized and motivated, and experience an intensely gratifying sense of purpose and meaning. During such times, we are vibrating at a high and expansive level of presence, expressing the unity between our spiritual essence and physical manifestation.

This is not always the case, however. When we pollute our minds with doubt, fear, or judgment, we lose connection to our highest purpose, and our actions fall out of alignment with our spiritual calling. As a result we vibrate at a much lower level of presence and may feel depressed, lost, or pessimistic.

Nature at Hand

Nature is a potent and readily available environment for realigning our spiritual essence in balance with its material expression. The stronger the presence of nature, the stronger its influence on our state of mind and our overall sense of harmony. This is why it is easy to become aware of our spiritual nature when we spend time in the wilderness. The same is true, to varying degrees, when we sit in a public park, work in our garden, or harvest vegetables that we have tenderly grown for months.

As different natural settings evoke different qualities of expansive sacredness, the more we are present to our natural surroundings, the more often we can access varying aspects of our spiritual essence. Walking on the beach by the ocean will evoke in us different qualities than climbing a mountain or spending time in our backyard. The scent and beauty of a rose will evoke different sensations than the scent of fresh herbs, and the beauty of a butterfly will awaken different qualities than the beauty of a fawn. The more we practice, the more we begin to notice these subtle differences and deepen our attunement to the sacredness of our being and the interconnectedness of life.

This power of nature is present also in the food we consume. As part of nature, vegetables, fruit, herbs, and green leaves emanate metaphysical properties in addition to their physical manifestation. The physical properties may be more obvious, but the metaphysical properties are equally present and just as real, even if we must develop a more subtle awareness in order to detect their presence.

Take, for instance, a lemon, which has a distinct taste and smell. The physical properties are apparent—the bright yellow color, the ovoid shape, and the pungent fragrance. If you were to peel off a piece of the skin and inhale its strong perfume, you would be inhaling the actual molecules of the lemon, traveling from the lemon peel through the air and into your nostrils. That is a physical phenomenon.

If you pay attention, you will find that the experience of smelling the peel of a lemon will evoke metaphysical responses in you as well. You might notice a shift in your thoughts as you think to yourself, "This is so refreshing. I feel uplifted." If you continue to pay attention, you might suddenly feel lighter and happy. These are the metaphysical properties of lemon, to which you gain access when you fully take in the experience of smelling a lemon.

It is easy to grasp the power of your interaction with nature through a lemon, as it is so potent, but the same is true, in more subtle ways, with every fruit and vegetable. It is easiest to experience when you eat plant-based food that has just been picked, as the physical and metaphysical properties are still potent. The more time that passes between the picking of the food and your consumption of it, the less vibrancy is present. That's why it is so healthy to eat food that is raw or slightly steamed rather than processed: the further the food is from its original vibrancy, the more its physical goodness and metaphysical qualities dissipate.

Even a few fresh leaves of an herb have the power to alter your mental and emotional state, connecting you to your spiritual essence. Take, for example, some fresh mint leaves and rub them in between your fingers. Absorb the scent and pay attention to what sensations, feelings, or thoughts are evoked in you. Then take a few lavender leaves and do the same. You will find that mint and lavender arouse very different sensations and qualities in you. Mint will probably awaken your spirit, while lavender might calm you. Whatever feelings you experience when inhaling or ingesting these herbs, you are connecting to an aspect of your spiritual essence through the physical and metaphysical properties of the herbs.

Now imagine adding some chopped mint leaves into a fruit salad, or some lavender leaves into a cup of warm milk with honey. Yes, this will enhance the flavor of your fruit salad and your warm milk and consequently your enjoyment of ingesting them, but it will also allow you to consume the metaphysical properties of the herbs with your food. You may experience a sense of awakening when tasting the mint in the fruit salad, and a sense of relaxation when savoring the taste of lavender in the milk. Even if you don't realize that these sensations are gifts from the herbs, they are doing their work to transport you to a greater and more sacred reality.

In this process of expanding your consciousness, you become aware of your interrelatedness to all things and the holiness and beauty of life. This is the power of nature and its accessibility. It can serve as a doorway to the hidden realm of existence—the realm of unconditional love and eternal life for which we all long.

The simple act of adding fresh herbs to our food can connect us to our spiritual essence, reminding us of the full range of our capacity to feel and experience. While we might not always be aware of it, nature's transformative power is always available to us. Remember, it is our attitude that changes, not nature itself. The more we become aware of our bond with nature, the more powerfully we will experience our connection to our spiritual essence and its expression in the world.

Finding the Four Keys in Nature

Spending time in nature offers an effective means with which to practice the Four Keys. Nature is expansive in all of its acts and moods, both the calmness of a sweet spring day and the blustering briskness of a winter storm. Every interaction with nature, therefore, is an opportunity to experience a distinct expansion of our sense of self. We seem to flow out of our accustomed bodily boundaries and into the natural surroundings—the grass, the branches of the trees, and the sounds of the birds. I experienced this expansiveness when I looked out the window at the beautiful English countryside while staying with my friend; the sense of awe and joy I felt at the beauty that lay before me transported me into the first key, *Expansive Presence*.

Once we have transcended our habitual state of mind, the multitude of sounds, scents, and sights in nature stir our thoughts and feelings and we enter a state of *Attentive Listening* where intuitive guidance may offer an insight or an understanding. Suddenly, observing a colony of ants may remind us to be more collaborative at work. Noticing two trees standing strong next to each other, their branches interwoven, may inspire us to evaluate the balance between separateness and connection in our relationships. In the instance of my English countryside vision, I gained an insight that nature is in perfect balance between its physical and spiritual properties. True to the nature of intuitive guidance, this insight announced itself, as if out of nowhere, as an obvious truth that, once revealed, could never again be denied.

Having received insight and guidance through attentive listening heightened by our time in nature, we may be motivated towards an *Inspired Action*: postponed e-mails may get written and the stack of bills and business matters addressed; some bogged-down portion of a project may be tackled with renewed enthusiasm; and we may return to our overall daily routine with a refreshed and more joyful attitude. After my insight regarding the perfect balance and unity present in nature, I was inspired to take many different actions, including sharing this perspective with others in my counseling work and professional writing.

Finally, nature is a paramount contributor to our *Faith-Filled Knowing*. Its unfailing ability to renew and refresh us is a constant reawakening to the realization that there is something greater in ourselves and our relation to the world—a truth that can be difficult to acknowledge when we are stuck in our constrictive, self-dictated routines and habits. In my case, the seemingly mundane moment of waking up in that countryside became profoundly sacred. I felt humbled that the Universe had chosen to open my eyes to the truth of nature's spiritual–material unity. This strengthened my belief that I was engaged in an intimate, ongoing relationship with the Divine Source.

We can access the Four Keys in any moment, regardless of the situation in which we find ourselves. Nature, however, offers a particularly powerful doorway through which to connect with our spiritual essence, awakening in us qualities that are equally present in the natural world and in each of us. Feeling renewed, grounded, and inspired, we bring these qualities into our daily choices and actions, creating unity between our spiritual intentions and material expressions.

Chapter 11

Aspire to Spiritual–Material Balance

I t is important to ground your spiritual development
in your material existence in order to balance the two.
To do that, you need to enhance your actions with spiritual qualities and values, as well as appreciate the material expression of your intentions and those of others.
Here are two guidelines to balancing the spiritual and
the material in all aspects of your life.

Guideline #1: Redefine Spiritual Fulfillment

Whenever you do something that connects you to your highest and most noble self, you experience spiritual fulfillment. You connect to your very best when you experience love and compassion for others, the free flow of your creative juices, a specific manifestation of your life purpose, or a deep sense of altruism and service to people in your life. This happens through daily activities that may seem ordinary and yet give you immense satisfaction and a sense of fulfillment. Spiritual fulfillment is often defined as something internal and separate from any external material factors, but such actions contain both a spiritual intention *and* a material expression.

For example, while you prepare a traditional weekend dinner for family and friends, you might think to yourself, "I love expressing my creativity and nourishing my family and friends through cooking and baking." As you look around the table, seeing everyone enjoy the food and conversation, you might say to yourself, "Another meal together, strengthening the ties between us." Later on, as everyone is helping to clean up, you might think, "It is worth all the time and hard work when I see how nourishing and fulfilling these weekly dinners are."

In the course of this seemingly ordinary event you've experienced your spiritual essence; qualities that express your highest, most noble self, like your creativity, your endless love and care, and your altruism; and something that gives you a sense of purpose.

In a work situation, you might be an accountant in a corporation. You're good with numbers and writing in neat columns, and when you present financial reports you take great pride in the care and diligence with which you prepare the data. Knowing that your professional attentiveness contributes to financial order and ease in the company, you feel a sense of purpose and service. At first this may seem like a purely mechanical and material endeavor, but if you pay attention to the sense of peace that comes over you when you organize the balance sheets and appreciate your contribution to the company, you will experience both fulfillment and satisfaction.

Guideline #2: Delight in the Material World

There are so many material things to appreciate and enjoy, from the beauty in nature to the usefulness of technology and the ingenuity of the arts, to mention just a few broad categories. Every artifact within these categories expresses a spiritual value and a material purpose. Many of these products are a manifestation of someone's life calling and higher purpose. So how can they be considered inferior because they are just material objects, when they are an expression of human creativity and ingenuity? Too often we tend to dismiss objects or discount experiences as being merely material, when in fact they are a manifestation of someone's self-expression.

Advancements in medical technology now allow people to live longer, and innovations in telecommunications permit us to connect across the globe. These are not purely material products; they entail such experiences as health, connection, livelihood, gratitude, care, and efficiency. They are a testament to the human spirit and require a new way of perceiving and interacting with what we have traditionally categorized as solely material.

The clothes you choose to wear can be an expression of different aspects of your personality, and you might choose what to wear according to your mood and purpose for the day. So buy your clothes with conscious intention and appreciate how fashion can help bring out different expressions of your individuality.

When you taste a new dish that awakens your palate in unusual ways, you benefit from the chef's creative spirit and years of hard work and dedication. This is not just a sensory experience, it is an exposure to imagination and originality. Also, when you are consuming someone else's creation, you are appreciating their inspiration and allowing them to fulfill their life calling.

All these are examples of objects and experiences that are usually considered superficially material. But if you take pleasure in them, appreciating their intrinsic qualities and the effort that went into creating them, you will experience the fulfillment and satisfaction that comes with living a life imbued with spiritual–material balance. It will elevate your vitality and the vibrancy of your world.

Epilogue

You're Off to Great Places . . .

You now hold the Keys to accessing the often hidden spiritual reality, and to fully integrating it into all aspects of your material daily living. Each of the Four Keys is a gateway to another layer of your human experience and expression in the world. Expanded Presence awakens you to a sacred awareness of yourself and everything around you. Attentive Listening provides you with guidance and inner wisdom drawn from a larger spiritual reality. Inspired Action channels your insights and inner promptings into a specific concrete manifestation. And Faith-Filled Knowing reinforces the expectation that a spiritual–material collaboration exists everywhere and is the formula for attaining personal and collective healing and wholeness.

Being aware of a spiritual reality and intentionally giving it expression while engaging in what formerly seemed mundane activities will open before you a whole new range of perceptions and experiences. Now that you are aware of the prevailing spiritual–material split which may once have fragmented so much of your life, you can begin to experience the spiritual components of your material existence and the physical manifestation of your spiritual nature.

Practicing gratitude and conscious breathing, engaging in authentic expression, and spending time in nature are some of the ways you can expand your consciousness and enter into union with this spiritual existence. In this state of mind, you can listen attentively and decipher subtle, intuitive information that can guide your choices and actions. All that remains for you to do is act upon this guidance with inspiration and determination, allowing the spiritual reality to penetrate and transform your ordinary, mundane life. As you do that, your faith will deepen and you will find that you have become a channel for wisdom to come through—transforming your world and the people whom you touch.

I am excited for you as you embark on this infinitely rewarding journey. May you find your way back home.

Acknowledgments

T hank you all who inspired, supported, and believed in me throughout the laborious process of birthing this book. It was not always easy to write about that which is so often beyond words. Each one of you helped bring this book into being.

I am infinitely grateful to you, Dorothy Maclean, Judy McAllister, Eileen Caddy, and the Findhorn community and education center, for your devotion to awakening people to the true nature of reality and the glorious possibilities of collaborating with the consciousness of nature. I heard the call and came to the two-week workshop "Falling in Love with God." Nothing was ever the same after that, and this book is my way to share the wisdom and knowledge that was passed on to me.

Leon, thank you for sharing your life with me, standing by me through everything, and loving me no matter what. Hari Meyers, without you this book would never have been completed. You were clearly sent by an angel to help me share my message with the world. Thank you for sitting next to me while I wrote, helping me think through complex ideas, encouraging me to include my personal story, and your hours of editing.

Thanks to all the coaches and editors who helped along the way, each moving me a step forward: Ann McIndoo, Steve Harrison and his Quantum Leap coaches Martha Bullen and Debra Englander, Robin Quinn, Mahesh Grossman, Patty Aubrey, and Jack Canfield. Thank you, Brooke Warner and She Writes Press, for trusting in me and my message.

Thank you to my friends and family—especially Mia Segal, Noel Canin, Hagit Cohen, Naomi Stoller, Stacey and Jonathan Fisher, Louisa Barnum, and Analesa Berg—for rooting for me all along, and for reading segments of the book and giving me honest and encouraging feedback. And most of all, thank you my dearest sons, Neder and Lev, for always inspiring me to make the world a better place for you and generations to come.

In gratitude,
Anna

About the Author

Anna Gatmon, PhD, comes from an eclectic background that spans the USA, Israel, Sweden and France. Her rich life journey has included careers as a fashion model, an educator and a counselor. Anna holds a Doctoral degree in Transformative Learning from the California Institute for Integral Studies. She is devoted to empowering people to transcend their personal and cultural suffering by living in spiritual and material harmony as the means to planetary healing and wholeness. Anna lives with her family in Sonoma County, California.

For more information about Anna Gatmon's work visit: www.annagatmon.com

Author photo © Rick English

Selected Titles from She Writes Press

She Writes Press is an independent publishing company founded to serve women writers everywhere. Visit us at www.shewritespress.com.

Note to Self: A Seven-Step Path to Gratitude and Growth by Laurie Buchanan. $16.95, 978-1-63152-113-3. Transforming intention into action, *Note to Self* equips you to shed your baggage, bridging the gap between where you are and where you want to be—body, mind, and spirit—and empowering you to step into joy-filled living *now!*

The Thriver's Edge: Seven Keys to Transform the Way You Live, Love, and Lead by Donna Stoneham. $16.95, 978-1-63152-980-1. A "coach in a book" from master executive coach and leadership expert Dr. Donna Stoneham, *The Thriver's Edge* outlines a practical road map to breaking free of the barriers keeping you from being everything you're capable of being.

Think Better. Live Better. 5 Steps to Create the Life You Deserve by Francine Huss. $16.95, 978-1-938314-66-7. With the help of this guide, readers will learn to cultivate more creative thoughts, realign their mindset, and gain a new perspective on life.

Renewable: One Woman's Search for Simplicity, Faithfulness, and Hope by Eileen Flanagan. $16.95, 978-1-63152-968-9. At age forty-nine, Eileen Flanagan had an aching feeling that she wasn't living up to her youthful ideals or potential, so she started trying to change the world—and in doing so, she found the courage to change her life.

Learning to Eat Along the Way by Margaret Bendet. $16.95, 978-1-63152-997-9. After interviewing an Indian holy man, newspaper reporter Margaret Bendet follows him in pursuit of enlightenment and ends up facing demons that were inside her all along.

Her Name Is Kaur: Sikh American Women Write About Love, Courage, and Faith edited by Meeta Kaur. $17.95, 978-1-938314-70-4. An eye-opening, multifaceted collection of essays by Sikh American women exploring the concept of love in the context of the modern landscape and influences that shape their lives.